A Christian Understanding of the
Human Person

Basic Readings

A Christian Understanding
of the
Human Person

Basic Readings

Edited by
Eugene Lauer
and Joel Mlecko

PAULIST PRESS   *New York/Ramsey*

Acknowledgements

The publisher wishes to gratefully acknowledge the use of the following materials: Excerpt from *The Religious Experience of Mankind* by Ninian Smart. Copyright © 1969 Ninian Smart. Reprinted by permission of Charles Scribner's Sons. Gregory Baum in *The Infallibility Debate,* ed. John Kirvan (New York: Paulist Press, 1971), pp. 9–13, 15. This material originally appeared in The *Ecumenist,* Vol. 9, No. 3, March/April 1971. Bernhard Lohse, *A Short History of Christian Doctrine* (Philadelphia: Fortress Press, 1966), pp. 8–12. Specified material abridged from pp. 276–282 in *The Religions of Man* by Huston Smith. Copyright © 1958 by Huston Smith. Reprinted by permission of Harper & Row, Publishers, Inc. From *Honest to God,* by John A. T. Robinson. © SCM Press Ltd. 1963. Published in the United States by The Westminster Press. Used by permission. Harvey Cox, "For Christ's Sake," *Playboy* Magazine 16 (January 1970), pp. 117, 122, 238–239. Karl Rahner, *Nature and Grace* (New York: Sheed and Ward, 1963), pp. 32–38. Excerpts from *The Human Adventure* by William McNamara. Copyright © 1974 by William McNamara. Reprinted by permission of Doubleday & Company, Inc. From *The Living God,* by Romano Guardini, translated by Stanley Godman. Copyright © 1957 by Pantheon Books, Inc. Reprinted by permission of Pantheon Books, a Division of Random House, Inc. George Martin, *Reading Scriptures as the Word of God* (Ann Arbor, Michigan: Servant Publications, 1975), pp. 28–30, 32–33, 60. George S. Worgul, "What Is a Sacrament?" *U.S. Catholic,* January 1977, pp. 29–31. Reprinted with permission from *U.S. Catholic,* published by Claretian Publications, 221 W. Madison St., Chicago, Ill. 60606. Bernard Häring, *The Law of Christ* (Westminster, Md.: Newman Press, 1963), Vol. 1, pp. 39–42. Michel Quoist, *Prayers* (New York: Sheed and Ward, 1963), pp. 61–63. Edward B. Fiske, "Saving the Earth: A Challenge to Our Religious Traditions," *Redbook,* June 1971, pp. 78, 180, 182, 186. *Small Is Beautiful* by E. F. Schumacher, pp. 18–19, 23–30, Frederick Muller Ltd. Publishers. Eugene Kennedy, "Sex and the Modern Christian," in *Sex: Thoughts for Contemporary Christians,* ed. Michael J. Taylor (Garden City, N.Y.: Doubleday, 1972), pp. 63–64, 66–74. Wolfhart Pannenberg, *What Is Man?* (Philadelphia: Fortress Press, 1970), pp. 110–113, 117–118. Excerpt from *Reaching Out* by Henri J. M. Nouwen. Copyright © 1975 by Henri J. M. Nouwen. Reprinted by permission of Doubleday & Comapny, Inc. *Theological Dimensions of the Liturgy* by Cyprian Vagaggini, pp. 277, 282, 284, 285–286, 293–295, 297. Published by The Liturgical Press, 1976. Copyrighted by The Order of St. Benedict, Inc. Collegeville, Minnesota. "The Church Today" (Chapter IV: The Life of the Political Community), Walter M. Abbott, ed., *The Documents of Vatican II* (New York: America Press, 1966) pp. 283–289. "On the Division Between Rich and Poor," in *Moral Issues and Christian Response* by Julius K. Nyerere and Paul T. Jersild (eds.) (Holt, Rinehart and Winston, New York). Reprinted by permission of Andre-Marie Dubarle, *The Biblical Doctrine of Original Sin,* London: Geoffrey Chapman and New York: Herder and Herder, 1964, pp. 224–226, 236–237, 244–245; © translation 1964, Geoffrey Chapman, a division of Cassell Ltd. Reprinted from *Christian Morality Today* by Charles Curran, with permission from the copyright holder, Fides/Claretian, 221 West Madison, Chicago, Illinois 60606. John F. O'Grady, *Christian Anthropology: A Meaning for Human Life* (New York: Paulist Press, 1976), pp. 118–123. Excerpts from *Contemplation in a World of Action* by Thomas Merton Copyright © 1965, 1969, 1970, 1971 by the Trustees of the Merton Legacy Trust. Reprinted by permission of Doubleday & Company, Inc. Specified material from pp. 17–20 in *The Living Temple: A Practical Theology of the Body and the Foods of the Earth* by Carl E. Braaten and LaVonne Braaten. Copyright © 1976 by Carl E. Braaten and LaVonne Braaten. Reprinted by permission of Harper & Row, Publishers, Inc. Marie Therese Ruthmann, "Celebrating Leisure Today," *Review for Religious* 32 (May 1973), pp. 544–548, 550–552, 556. Elisabeth Kübler Ross *et al.,* "Foreword" and "Omega" in *Death: The Final Stage of Growth* (Englewood Cliffs: Prentice-Hall, 1975), pp. x–xiii and 164–167.

Contents

V Relationship with Others

VI Relationship with Self

Introduction

What does it mean to be a human person from a Christian perspective? The specific answers to that question have varied from generation to generation. In the Gospel of John (10:10), Jesus stated, "I have come that you may have life and have it more abundantly." St. Irenaeus in the second century pointed out that the glory of God is indeed a human being who is fully alive. We, your editors, concur. Further, we maintain that Christian personning—or becoming a human person who is fully alive—preeminently involves relationships. The "I" does not exist alone; it is only in the context of relationships that the "I" is defined. Each one of us can unhesitatingly exclaim: because you are, I am. The relationships in which we all are involved are intertwining, energizing, and they often provide us with more adventure than clarity.

It is our position that there are only what we have termed the "four basic relationships." They include all the possible relationships in which we are involved and through which we become fully human:

1. relationship of the person with the Other or God;
2. relationship of the person with the material world;
3. relationship of the person with other human persons;
4. relationship of the person with the self.

For a Christian, all these relationships are epitomized and vitalized by the potent example of Jesus the Christ. That potent example was and is experienced by people as they enter into the life and teachings of Jesus. And that potent example is reflected by the followers of Jesus, by Christian persons.

It is our contention that to be born into a Christian family is not to be a Christian person. To simply know and parrot doctrines and ethical principles of Christianity is not to be a Christian person. We

1

maintain that being a Christian person is the recognition, appreciation, and acceptance of the four basic relationships, understood in
the context of the life and teachings of Jesus the Christ:

   —a recognition that the four basic relationships do indeed exist;
   —an appreciation of these relationships as necessary for Christian personning;
   —an acceptance of one's responsibilities to continually grow in
these relationships and to facilitate the growth of others in these relationships, primarily by one's own life-example.

   These three elements of recognition, appreciation, and acceptance of the four basic relationships form a consecutive process; that
is, one flows out of the other and leads to the next in a continually
spiralling fashion.
   On the other hand, the four basic relationships form not a consecutive process but an integral experience; that is, being involved in
one relationship means being involved in all the relationships. The
adult Christian cannot say, for example, "I'll get it together with myself and then I'll take care of my relationship with others." Nor can
the adult Christian say, "I'll take care of my relationship with others
and then I'll take care of God." Rather, adult Christians "get it all
together" with self only insofar as they relate to others, to the surrounding material world, and to God. And they "get it all together"
with God only insofar as they relate to self, others, and the world. In
a word, we do not work on one relationship and then move on to the
next; the four basic relationships are delicately interdependent. The
relationships are concomitant; they are being engaged at the same
time, on various levels of subtlety. The Christian Scriptures confirm
this view when they tell us that anyone who says he loves God and
hates his neighbor is a liar, or that whoever gives a cup of water to a
person in need gives it also to Christ. Certainly, becoming a fully
alive human person is not simply our own doing. It is also the work
of God who addresses us by means of the relationships of life, but it
is up to us to respond to those relationships.
   We can ask here which of the four basic relationships is most
important. Theoretically, we might build a strong argument for the
relationship with the Other or God. Existentially, however, we suggest that the relative importance of any one relationship depends on
the moment—on what we are called to be and to do in this particular
situation, with its uniquely relational component. Indeed, focusing
well on any one relationship will open us to the other three relation-

ships. For example, in this anthology we treat contemplation under the relationship with the Other. In contemplation of God, however, we are involved in the three other relationships. The material world around us, in which we sense the mystery of God's presence, is a trigger for our contemplation of God; and the attitude gained from contemplation fashions a unique facet of my self-understanding and thereby facilitates, enchances, and vitalizes my relationship with others.

Experience and most assuredly the Bible affirm that we humans are relational, as is all of reality. The basic ideas of the Bible—God, humans, love, hate, sin, conversion, covenant, fidelity—are relational at their core. I, an individual, am not alone in this world; I am a person-in-relationships.

We are discussing the art of Christian personning in the context of living relationships—not in the context of static, unchanging categories. We are, therefore, implying the necessity of dynamism and process. That is, how we live today is subject to change and growth tomorrow, in the light of our personal—and of humanity's—experience and understanding. Being a person-in-relationships is not something static. Living or believing today just how we lived and what we believed ten years ago may well be an indication not of spiritual health, or of Christian personning, but of spiritual stagnation and human diminution. Relationships are living realities. There is no such thing as a static relationship. If tomorrow it is as you left it the day before, that relationship has died a little. Being a person-in-relationships implies a lifelong process of growth and development into a deeper, vaster, maturing network of the four basic relationships.

During the past almost two thousand years, Christian theology—and therefore Christian personning—has at times ignored one or another of the four basic relationships or has overemphasized one relationship to the detriment of the others. Recent examples of this in the United States are striking. In the 1960's some Christians emphasized the relationship with others through involvement with social protest and social improvement movements, whereas in the early 1970's there was an emphasis on the relationship with the Divine, as witnessed by the Jesus and charismatic movements. The 1980's have yet to unfold. Various schools of theologizing, various courses, books, and approaches to Christian personning have emphasized one or another of the four basic relationships but not, to our knowledge, a delicate balancing of all the four basic relationships.

Our anthology attempts to represent the best of a wide spectrum of recent, mainly Christian theological, writings which, taken as a whole, do illuminate and provide a delicate blending of the four basic relationships. Naturally, and thankfully, no anthology is without its critics. Some of you will dispute the appropriateness of the topics we have chosen and what we did not choose. No anthology is exhaustive. Good and relevant material is often omitted simply because of lack of space—and because of lack of time. (When is the time for practicing the message if we spend all our time reading about the message!) Further, where we have placed our selections may seem arbitrary to others of you. We did attempt to situate topics in those relationships where the topics would bring out a sound modern emphasis in theology, where they might correct some past misemphasis, and where they would strike a person as being immediately meaningful.

Where, for example, would you include the topic of "sin"—relationship with the Other, with others, with self, with the material world? In the relational context in which we are speaking, we could say that sin is a grasping at, and clinging to, one of the relationships to the exclusion of the other three. Thus, we can perceive that it is a non-integral human experience (that is, sin) to get so attached to material progress that we have little time for developing friendships; or, it is simply disruptive (that is, sinful) to be so fanatical in the pursuit of God that we begin to destroy our physical and mental health. Traditionally, we have referred to sin as an offense against God; and most of us would, therefore, think of it primarily in the relationship with the Other. In that frame of reference, we have unfortunately developed a semantic about "hurting God" and about "pleasing God," with the expectation of a reward. To challenge this misdirection, we include sin under the relationship with the self in order to emphasize a most basic notion that sin is a disruption of self, that sin limits and contracts us rather than expanding and developing us.

Another example: under which relationship would you place "liturgy"? In line with the best spirit of the contemporary liturgical movement most people would judge, with us, that liturgy should be included under the relationships with others. In some Christian traditions where "going to church" was such a "me and God" experience, there is a real need to highlight the fact that Christian worship is intended to do more than put one in a good relationship with God. Christians must lift one another up in prayer, must experience the great support that comes from being strengthened by the prayer of others. Placing liturgy under the relationship with others can also help to address that age-old bromide-misconception that so many people use as an excuse for not participating in any communal worship, viz., "I don't get anything out of it." That statement is literally putting liturgy solely under the relationship with self, to the exclusion of the other three relationships.

Sharing this anthology as course material for several years on the college level has confirmed the validity of our initial theological intuition in choice and arrangement of material. Sharing these materials in this arrangement has flowed pedagogically and has received student approbation. Of course, we must recall once again that even though material is placed in one relationship, that does not mean it has no connection with other relationships. Remember, the four basic relationships are an integral experience.

We believe the value of the four basic relationships for a Christian understanding of the human person—and for the art of Christian personning—lies in their being a concise, precise, and all-embracing measure for both understanding and evaluating one's own religious development. Further, the construct of the four basic relationships provides an intellectually respectful introduction into how one would go about approaching personning from any perspective, philosophical or religious—without getting bogged down in methodological issues.

We ask you, the reader, to confront this model of the four basic relationships and this anthology with your own questions, arising from your personality and your concerns. Thus, this material and your questioning will form a relationship between us and also will form a model for balanced theologizing and for healthy Christian personning.

We trust that our dialogue will enthuse and guide you to other resources—books, articles, persons—and to practice. We hope, through our paradigm of the four basic relationships, to stimulate prayerful reflection on and practice of what the Christian community believes is important for becoming a full human person—important, that is, for the art of Christian personning.

I
The Role of Religion
in Becoming Human

Introduction

In noting the ubiquity and variety of religion, a person might well ask: Why does religion exist? The responses are numerous. Religion provides a context for reverencing divinity; religion offers solace in times of emotional turmoil; religion forces crisis in order to raise consciousness; religion excites our capacity for wonder and awe in the face of life's possibilities. We, your editors, particularly favor the response that religion facilitates the ability of its adherents to face reality, to find meaning in reality, and thereby, to live life more fully—to become more human.

Religion accomplishes that purpose and task through the various dimensions of religion: ritual, doctrine, ethics, Scripture, prayer, and so on. All these dimensions have their source and goal in religious experience: a life-transforming encounter with divinity. Jesus, for example, had a religious experience; his encounter with God was so intense and intimate that he called God "Father." That religious experience not only transformed his life but also the lives of generations after him. For Jesus' religious experience became the source for the dimensions of Christian ritual, doctrine, ethics, Scripture, and prayer. And the goal of those Christian dimensions is to lead the followers of Jesus to an experience of God similar to that of their exemplar, Jesus. Through that experience, those followers will be able to face reality, to find meaning in reality, and thereby to live life more fully, just as Jesus did.

You do not have to be personally religious to appreciate the fact that religion plays a central role in human history and human behavior. In the theist's acceptance of religion and the atheist's rejection of religion, we human persons have expressed some of our deepest feelings and most basic values not only toward divinity but also toward the material world, other human beings, and our own individual selves. The influence of religion has been powerful on governments, education, the arts—in a word, on the lives and behavior of billions of people.

Thus, religion is much more than a way of believing; it is a way of living. Religion deals with basic questions which all adults somehow and at some time in their lives ask themselves:

—Who am I?
—What is the purpose of my life?
—Is this all there is?
—What's it all about?

These questions cannot be suppressed by consumer goods, drugs, or totalitarian governments. These are basic questions which seem to arise from the very nature of our being. They have to be thought out and their answers lived if one is to live life more fully, if one is to become more human.

Religion, and the religious person, is not satisfied with life as it is given. The religious person seeks the fulfillment of life in the context of the very best, the ultimate. Religious persons like Moses, Muhammad, and Jesus have striven to live life at the zenith, to reach the "unreachable." Are such persons hopelessly deluded or are they the only truly sane? Each one of us is living out the answer to that question as we struggle to become more and more human.

1
Overview of Religions
Ninian Smart

Ninian Smart is professor of religious studies at the University of Lancaster in England. He studied at Oxford and lectured at Yale and the University of Wisconsin. Smart is well known for his books, among them *World Religions: A Dialogue, Philosophers and Religious Truth, The Yogi and the Devotee,* and *The Religious Experience of Mankind,* from which the following selection is excerpted.

In order to understand religion, it is necessary to understand religions or to sense the multiplicity of mankind's religious life. A summary of religions, such as Ninian Smart offers us in the following excerpt, provides us a perspective for viewing religion as a manifestation of the human spirit, which manifestation is to be found in all geographical areas and in every age. Further, such a summary provides Christians an opportunity to formulate an initial response to our religiously pluralistic world.

One possible Christian response to the fact of many religions in the world is *exclusivism:* only Christianity is true, other religions are false. A second response is *fulfillment:* other religions are not false but incomplete and preparatory for the final revelation of Christianity. Another response is *pluralism:* the various religions are diverse paths leading to a single goal, just as many different roads ascend a mountain from different sides and finally meet at the top.

A fourth response—and seemingly fruitful one, particularly in the context of the four basic relationships—is *dialogic.* This response entails neither an attack on another religion nor a repudiation of the distinctive orientation of one's own religion. Rather, the dialogic response entails dialogue: listening to, and learning from, the other religious believer and explaining one's own religious position, through words and actions, that is, by living one's religion. The dialogue partners deepen one another's understanding: they probe, possibly reconceive, and hopefully enhance their own religious beliefs.

In such a dialogue, Christians might learn something from the strict simplicity and brotherhood within Islam. Christians might balance their anthropomorphic ideas of God in the light of the transpersonal understanding of the Other in Buddhism. From Confucianism, Christians might develop a deeper appreciation of the here-and-now vis-à-vis overconcern with the hereafter.

Of course, in the dialogic response a Christian keeps in mind the belief in universal salvation. In the Gospel of Matthew (7:21) Jesus remarks to his disciples that it is not enough simply to acknowledge him as Lord in order to enter the kingdom of heaven. It is necessary to do the will of the Father. In Matthew (25:31–46) we find the well-known sketch of that will. It is Judgment Day. Those who have cared for the hungry, sick, imprisoned, and those in need are called into the kingdom, and those who have ignored those in need are excluded. Whether or not they have recognized Jesus as Lord and Savior is not the key factor. Certainly, our Christian knowledge of God through Jesus and through the Christian community is not in itself a ticket to heaven. Such knowledge simply places greater demands on us to be open, responsible, and loving—key qualities in any dialogic relationship.

How religion started we cannot tell for certain. . . . There is ample evidence that religious rites were practiced in early prehistoric times and it may well be that the sense of the sacred has been part of man's experience from the very beginning. It is notable that before the emergence of the human species proper (homo sapiens), Neanderthal Man—some 150,000 years ago—practiced the ritual interment of the dead. This seems to point to a belief in an afterlife of some kind and to belief in an "invisible" world.

A dramatic turning point in man's history occurred between 4000 and 3000 B.C. in the Middle East, with the beginnings of urban civilization. In the latter part of the fourth millennium B.C., a settled agricultural life in the more fertile areas of Egypt and Mesopotamia provided the resources for the establishment of cities, which in turn allowed not only centralization of civil and religious administration, but also the growth of elaborate temple cults and of an organized priesthood. The discovery of writing had by then created a profound change in man's life. Written words gradually came to replace memory as the source of tradition, and provided a creative means of expressing man's religious heritage. Egypt and Mesopotamia became centers of civilization, and further east, in the Indus Valley, in northwest India, and in China, there developed important cultures.

It is no accident, perhaps, that from these three areas—the Middle East, India, and China—the three great sources of the world religions evolved. It is curious, in this connection, that between a three-hundred-year span, 800 to 500 B.C., the great religious traditions of the world crystallized. In Palestine there occurred the decisive emergence of a monotheistic faith through the work of the Hebrew prophets; the Judaism they developed became the foundation upon which both Christianity and Islam were later built. In India this was the period of the composition of the most important of the Upanishads—the writings that form part of the sacred scripture of Hinduism. The Upanishads contain germinally the ideas later elaborated in the various theologies that remain to this day the forms under which the Hindu sees the world about him.

During the same three hundred years, unorthodox teachers in India challenged the tradition of the Aryans who had invaded India during the second millennium B.C. and whose beliefs, rituals, and social structure had long dominated north India. Two of these unorthodox teachers have lived in the memory of religious people until today: Mahavira, the "jina" or "Conqueror," who restored an archaic tradition of religious belief, and whose teachings are handed down today in the faith known as Jainism; and the Buddha, the "Enlightened One."

Both lived in the sixth century B.C. Though Jainism has diminished to less than two million people at the last census—there are only a handful of Jains outside India—Buddhism has been the most successful missionary religion, at least statistically, that the world has seen. Buddhism spread to Ceylon, Burma, and Southeast Asia . . . and it also penetrated into China, Tibet, Mongolia, Korea, and Japan. . . . It is no exaggeration to say that the whole of the East Asian continental mass has been permeated or influenced by Buddhism, with the exception of Siberia. In brief, Buddhism has become a major world force: Jainism has remained, with ups and downs, a religion of the Indian subcontinent. Admittedly, by about 1100 A.D. Buddhism was virtually finished in its homeland; but like Christianity, which also did not take root in its place of origin, Buddhism spread far and wide. There are currently Buddhist missions in Europe and the United States; nor are they without success.

　. . . Confucius who lived approximately from 551 to 479 B.C. . . . reformed, clarified, and systematized the earlier traditions of China into a coherent social and religious system. The Confucian ethic has remained until this day a powerful factor in Chinese culture, both at home and overseas. A legendary contemporary (many scholars dispute his existence and date) Lao-Tse, whose more mystical and contemplative teachings are summed up in the *Tao-Te-Ching* (*The Classic of the Tao and Its Power*), was the source of a religion which has also had profound influence upon Chinese life. Though Taoism may now be in a state of deep decline, it not only was a powerful cultural and spiritual force, but it also had an effect on Buddhism when that religion came to evangelize China. Zen Buddhism is indeed the Japanese form of a movement which represents a blend between Taoist and Buddhist ideas and contemplative techniques.

　In China three religions were dominant through most of the period from the second century A.D. until modern times—Confucianism, Taoism, and Buddhism. In Japan, through the cultural influence of China, Confucianism and Buddhism came to permeate Japanese life. But the indigenous faith, Shinto (the Way of the Gods), survived the intrusion. Although Shinto was used by militarists in the period preceding and during World War II to promote nationalism, this was in effect a distortion of its values, and certainly it continues to be important in Japanese life.

　Let us now make a few further observations on the development of religions in the Western and Middle Eastern world. Some time about the sixth century B.C. or earlier, the prophet Zoroaster was preaching an ethical monotheism based on the principle that there is a cosmic struggle between the supreme Good Spirit (Ahura Mazda) and the Evil Spirit (Angra Mainyu). In so doing, Zoroaster, or more correctly, Zarathustra, transcended the existing polytheistic faith which was closely related to that of the Aryans who invaded India. Further west, the Hebrew people became the first of all the Semitic peoples occupying the area from Egypt to Mesopotamia to attain a true monotheism. (Akhenaten in Egypt, during the twelfth century B.C., had attempted to elevate Aten to solitary and exclusive godhood over the various gods of a complex polytheism, but the attempt was unsuccessful and after his death the traditional rituals were restored.) Jewish monotheism might not have achieved an important place in the ancient world had it not been transformed through the life of Christ and the subsequent spread of Christianity through most of the Middle East and Graeco-Roman world. In all probability, Jewish monotheism would otherwise have remained the faith of a minor nation within the structure of the Roman Empire.

Christianity had spectacular success in converting Europe, North Africa, and the Middle East, and by the fourth century A.D. became the official religion of the Empire. Thereafter, its onward course was checkered. Over a period of centuries, the Eastern Church, centered in Byzantium, and the Western Church, headed by the Pope in Rome, grew apart. In the seventh century A.D., the teachings of Muhammad began to spread explosively beyond his Arabian homeland, and in fifty years Islam was the dominant faith of North Africa, a large part of Spain, nearly all the Middle East, and parts of Central Asia. From the eleventh century, it penetrated into India, and in the fifteenth, finally destroyed the Byzantine Empire, thereby gaining an entrance into eastern Europe. In the early part of the sixteenth century, Luther sparked off the Reformation, so that Christendom split into three main segments—Roman Catholic, Protestant, and Eastern Orthodox. This division has continued to the present time, though there are now powerful forces at work to bring about reunion.

Christianity lost many adherents through the impact of Islam in the Middle Ages. In the Renaissance, though internal divisions hampered it, a new era of expansion opened up for Christendom with the navigational successes of the sea-going nations of Europe. The discoveries of the New World and of the sea-route to India and beyond gave Christian missionaries amazing opportunities. Moreover, the settlements in North America, Australia, and New Zealand by European people, and the conquest of Latin America, naturally meant that Christian culture was to dominate these areas. Though missions had some success in Asia, the population on the whole remained loyal to the long-established traditional faiths.

SOURCE: Ninian Smart, *The Religious Experience of Mankind* (New York: Charles Scribner's Sons, 1969), pp. 18–21.

2
Theological Method
Gregory Baum

All religions make use of some form of theology, that is, a systematic reflection on data that the adherent of a religion believes to be of essential importance in living life. That data of theology is believed by the adherent to have been divinely revealed whereas the data of philosophy, for example, has a human origin. For the believer, therefore, the revealed data of theology has radical value due to its divine source. The endeavor of theology is to uncover that value of the data for each new generation and for varying cultural contexts.

The core datum of theology (theos = god, logos = study of) is, of course, the Other or God. By definition, God is never completely knowable; for God is mystery—not unknowable, but *infinitely* knowable. God is mystery which can be plumbed but never completely exhausted. This being so, theology must be marked by dynamism, a constant questioning and probing, a creative tension—almost a dissatisfaction between what is known about God and what can be known.

Since individuals necessarily approach God from their own unique perspectives, there will never be a single theology in a healthy religion. There must be theologies. At the same time, theology must be done in a context broader than the immediate experience of the individual. Individuals must be open not only to their experience but to that of others, in and out of their own religious tradition—past and present. Further, they must be aware of human striving in other disciplines, for example physics and psychology, which also are the areas of God's activity. Parameters must not—and cannot—be placed around the activity of God.

Because theology expresses itself in the idiom of its historical occurrence, we must beware of taking too literally or absolutely any theology, from wherever or whomever, as the final wording for understanding God. Creeds, dogmas, council statements, theological images of God—even Scripture itself—have to be interpreted anew in each age. The sacred, orthodox, or theological words are not the major concern; understanding and experience of God is the major concern, and sometimes words can get in the way of that understanding and experience.

In the following excerpt from the book *The Infallibility Debate,* Gregory Baum gives some excellent insights into this problem of taking the wording of any one theological school too literally. Baum's writing was occasioned by the theological reaction to the well-known Swiss theologian Hans Küng's book, *Infallible? An Inquiry.* The prominent German theologian Karl Rahner took exception to some of the assertions made by Küng in that book. The prime area of conflict is how one interprets the Bible as the source for the present expression of Christian teaching. In other words, their confrontation centered on *theological method.*

Küng has the tendency to emphasize biblical witness in any Christian teaching and constantly calls one to return to biblical thought patterns. Rahner points out forcefully the need to reinterpret in every age the meaning of that historical biblical witness. Baum compares the probing and questioning of these two theological approaches in our excerpt and tries to glean the value that is present in each of them.

Gregory Baum is professor of theology at St. Michael's, University of Toronto, and editor of the prestigious journal of ecumenical studies, *The Ecumenist.*

Despite the mistakes, the Church remains in God's truth. This is Küng's position. But how is the Church maintained in this truth? In part, as we have seen, through creedal statements summing up the story of salvation and through defensive statements excluding certain choices as going against the Gospel. But the main source of the Church's truth is the Bible. Hans Küng does not deny that the Scriptures must also be studied as historical documents, that they also contain errors, and that they also utter the divine message with presuppositions and through concepts that are no longer our own. They, too, are in need of reinterpretation.

At the same time, Küng adopts very strong language to express the pre-eminent place of the Bible in the Church. He calls it the *norma normans non normata.* The Bible is the measure of truth, itself unmeasured, measuring all other statements of faith. This expression, taken from traditional Lutheran theology, has acquired considerable importance in recent ecumenical discussions in Germany. To assure Lutherans that the Catholic stress on tradition does not mean the addition of new truths of faith nor belittle the Bible as the one source of faith, many Catholic theologians have adopted this phrase. At moments of ecumenical fervor I have made use of the expression myself. It is, however, a most unfortunate phrase. It was originally a rhetorical overstatement, an expression of piety, a fervent claim to be independent of tradition. Yet the Bible, despite its pre-eminent position, is not the measure, itself unmeasured, measuring all other truth. This is not how the Bible is actually used in the Churches. Throughout their life and history the Churches actually have determined what the center of the Scriptures is, and they read the entire Scriptures in the light of this central message and concern. The Bible is never a book situated in empty space. It is always found in a Church that already exists, that has a doctrinal tradition, a certain liturgy, institutions of various kinds and a definite tie to a particular culture. While the Scriptures do exercise a normative function in the Churches, the use of such a rhetorical expression obscures the difficult problem of how the Churches have actually determined the center of the Gospel, in the light of which they understand the Scriptures and their entire past.

At certain places Hans Küng makes claims for the Scriptures that seem excessive to me. He wants to relativize the dogmas of the Church in respect to the abiding, unchanging norm of Jesus Christ as present to us in the New Testament. But the New Testament itself is an historical document and hence in need of reinterpretation. At this point fruitful conversation between [the theologians Hans] Küng and [Karl] Rahner must continue. . . .

Before analyzing Rahner's response to Küng, let me explain the difference between the theological approaches these two men have adopted from the very beginning of their work. Küng and Rahner represent two contrasting currents in Catholic theology. Both theologians affirm the need for the reform of Church life and the renewal of doctrine. Küng's tendency is to stress the biblical witness, to conceive of renewal in the Church as a biblical critique of present teaching and practice, and to advocate the closest possible conformity of the Church to the New Testament ideal. While Küng does not deny that later developments in the Church may have been necessary, good and useful, he regards these developments as purely human; they remain for him under the judgment of the biblical norm. Much of Küng's brilliant theological and historical research has brought out the problematic character of post-biblical developments in the Church and demonstrated how enlightening and powerful the biblical message remains in the present situation.

Karl Rahner also regards the Scriptures as a normative witness for the entire life of the Church, but he holds—and he is followed in this by a great number of contemporary theologians—that the significant post-biblical, doctrinal and institutional developments, while never wholly without sin or free of human failing, may nonetheless represent God's revelatory action in the Church. This divine action is God's ongoing self-communication to the Christian community, which enables the Church to interpret the Scriptures as God's Word addressed to her in the present and to adapt her institutional life to the needs of the Christian fellowship. Thus the Church is faithful to the divine message, once and for all revealed in Christ to the apostles, only as she continues to interpret it out of her present salvational situation. To reform the Church and renew her doctrine, therefore, it is not necessary to return to the biblical models of institutional life and linguistic expressions. What is important is to reinterpret the witness of Scripture and past tradition so that God's gift of himself as Word and Spirit be made available to people in institutions that embody their present self-understanding and in concepts drawn from their contemporary experience of reality.

While Küng has always been concerned with honesty, truth and error in the Church, Rahner has been much more interested in the historicity of all truth. Rahner has brilliantly shown that a doctrinal statement, made at a particular moment in the Church's life, has built into it historical presuppositions and philosophical concepts, and that the Christian witness of such a statement is made available to us only as we understand the historical circumstances of its first formulation. For while presuppositions and conceptuality are the vessels of the witness of faith, they themselves need not be part of it, they do not oblige later generations, and they may be left behind not simply as outdated but even, possibly, as erroneous. What is important for the Church is to reaffirm in the present the Christian witness present in the doctrinal statement, and this can be done only in terms and concepts drawn from contemporary experience and based on presuppositions that are critically examined. If truth is historical, then the truth of a doctrine cannot be preserved simply by repeating it; to protect and promote the truth, the doctrine must again and again be reinterpreted in the Church's ongoing history. Rahner has never taught that dogmas are immutable in the Church. On the contrary, he has always taught that the only way to remain faithful to the Church's dogma is to reformulate and reconceptualize it in the present. Almost his entire theological work, vast as it is, has been dedicated to the faithful reinterpretation of dogma, self-identical with iself and yet new, powerful, relevant. . . .

Rahner admits that dogmas may become "erroneous"; by this he means that the questions to which these dogmas replied and the conceptuality in which they were formulated may change, and that by repeating these dogmas in literal fashion at a later time, we may in fact be saying something the dogmas never intended, something that has little to do with the Gospel, something that is wrong. The task of the theologian, Rahner repeats, is precisely to reinterpret the original dogma so that the divine truth proclaimed in it (not its literal meaning) can be uttered in the contemporary Church where other crucial questions have arisen and where other concepts are used to understand reality. . . .

SOURCE: Gregory Baum in *The Infallibility Debate,* ed. John J. Kirvan (New York: Paulist Press, 1971), pp. 9–13, 15.

3
Theology: Evolving Process
Bernhard Lohse

Did Jesus of Nazareth give a revelation in a set of precise statements that were to be passed down, untouched and untampered with, until his second coming? Hardly, for such a process would be inhuman. We human beings simply do not function that way. It is not reasonable to expect that God would self-reveal to us in a manner that is in direct contradiction to the way he created us. God created all persons as thinking, evolving, growing beings. To give us a static set of revealed propositions, firmly encased in one set of terms in one language for all time, would be a shock to our nervous systems as well as to our minds and hearts.

We Christians indeed believe that God self-reveals in and through Christ, and that this revelation is faithfully written down in the Christian Scriptures. However, Christians do not believe that the Scriptures capture the total content of that revelation in a single reading. They gradually discover and unfold the riches of that content through generations of effort and search, experiment and re-evaluation. (And this is exactly in tune with the way that human nature is. We are curious, seeking, excitable, wide-eyed creatures who are always yearning to learn more, to understand better.) Each generation comes up with, through the guidance of the Holy Spirit, a new insight into the original revelation that was not in the consciousness of believers before them. Future generations will, under the guidance of the same Spirit, come to new awareness of the meaning of revelation that we today never thought of.

Theology is, therefore, a process—a process of discovering and unfolding the meaning of revelation. Dogmas are statements of the present understanding of that unfolding process.

In the selection that follows, Bernhard Lohse, professor of historical theology at the University of Hamburg, explains how this unfolding process takes place. His primary emphasis is on the fact that human believers will always sense a need to express their faith, to put what they believe onto concrete language, into meaningful summaries, to develop "confessions." "Confessions" are attempts by believers to say as clearly and as directly as they can, "This is what I believe and am committed to."

The instinctive need to pray was another reason why there was a development of the initial biblical revelation. Human persons could not just repeat for generation after generation the prayer formulas of the Scriptures. By nature we are creative beings, persons who tend to go beyond what we have learned in our youth. When we get wrapped up in the act of speaking with God, we want to say more about the relationship, to address God more intimately, more individually according to the new circumstances that we are in. At the same time, faithful believers take great pains to be sure that what they are saying is in accord with what God has revealed. For example, Christians began to address Jesus directly as "Our Lord God" only after they felt reasonably sure that this was an accurate and fitting expression of what was contained in the Gospels.

Finally, Lohse points out why there must be a *continuity* in the evolution of Christian theology and dogmatic expression. We will oversimplify it—it is the task of believers to understand a revelation, not to create one. It is the goal of believers to dig deeply into revelation to discover its riches, not to think out issues so brilliantly that we ourselves come up with "brand new" answers. Rather we come up with "new understandings" of the Christian tradition, insights that were not previously in human consciousness. In this sense, the ideas are genuinely fresh and new and lead us on pathways not yet traversed.

John Henry Newman, a great nineteenth-century Christian thinker from England, explained the issue of continuity very simply by comparing the unfolding of Christian doctrine to the growth of a flower. In seed form, one cannot perceive directly the magnificence of color and shape and odor of the full blossom. Yet it *is* all there in the seed. Only through careful nurturing does the full content of the flower come to be manifest to all. When fully grown, it has not become something completely different from its seed stage; it has simply unfolded what was already there. So it is with Christian teaching. Each generation will continue to "water the seeds" and see them unfold in ways that will have an eternal freshness.

If one thinks of dogmas as confessions, or doctrinal confessions, it should be possible to find a satisfactory answer to the difficult question of the inception of the history of dogma as well as of its further development. As far as the inception of the history of dogma is concerned, there is no doubt that Jesus made a unique claim, that he was not satisfied with the mere attempt to instruct men concerning this teaching or that, but, instead, challenged them to commit themselves to him, i.e., to confess him. In this sense confessions existed during the earthly ministry of Jesus. According to the Gospel of Matthew (16:15) Jesus asked his disciples, "Who do you say that I am?" It is immaterial whether or not Jesus actually put this question to his disciples at a specific point in his career. What this account from Matthew makes strikingly clear is the goal toward which Jesus directed his entire proclamation, namely commitment to him, or confession of him. The answer Peter gives to this question from Jesus—"You are the Christ, the Son of the living God"—is the first dogma, then, in the sense of a confession.

Since this confession by Peter there has never been a time when Christians did not face the task of expressing their faith in the form of a confession. For various reasons, however, such confession was not merely repeated in the short and simple form in which Peter made it but was further expanded and more fully articulated. The first and most important reason for the fuller elaboration of confession, as well as for the development of doctrine, at least at the beginning, is the fact that very soon after the crucifixion and resurrection of Jesus the primitive community began to pray to its exalted Lord. This is a fact the significance of which can hardly be overestimated. That the primitive Christian community was given to this custom from its earliest days is attested by the Aramaic prayer *Maranatha* preserved in 1 Cor. 16:22 and by the prayer of Paul in 2 Cor. 12:8 as well as by other instances (cf. Acts 9:14; Rom. 10:12–14; 1 Cor. 1:2). Prayers can be addressed only to God. If they are addressed to Jesus Christ, therefore, the question concerning the relationship of the exalted Lord to God necessarily arises. Hence the development of the dogma of the Trinity and of Christology has its beginnings in the early days of the church, even though it took a long time before a doctrine was actually formulated.

Additional reasons can be given for the development of dogmas and confessions. There was, of course, no lack of opportunities to confess one's faith in connection with such events as baptism, the celebration of the Lord's Supper, the proclamation of the gospel, and especially the carrying out of the church's mission. In addition, the fact that the Christian faith often encountered opposition frequently led to new confessions, or at least to an expansion of the existing affirmations of faith. Among the various other reasons which might also be cited is the significant role that philosophy later played in the development of dogma and especially in its interpretation. Certain problems were progressively clarified with the help of philosophical conceptualization. Finally, it should be noted that at times dogma also manifested a tendency toward self-expansion, with new questions being answered by analogy to similar problems that had already found a solution.

It would be hard to deny that under these circumstances dogmas, or doctrinal confessions, at times moved far, sometimes very far, from their beginnings in the New Testament. And yet it is true that the Christian faith could at no time refrain from creating confessions. Confession is by its very nature an essential element of faith. No matter how critically specific dogmas or doctrinal confessions of Christianity may be viewed, this fundamental principle cannot be denied on the basis of the New Testament. Melanchthon, in his *Apology of the Augsburg Confession,* said correctly: "No faith is firm that does not show itself in confession." It must be admitted that confession may lead to an externalizing and formalizing of the faith, and that occasionally this has been the case. Still the fact remains that faith without dogma, without confession, is continually in danger of no longer knowing what it really believes, and therefore of falling to the level of mere religiosity.

The continuity in the development of the history of dogma does not show itself only when one compares the beginnings of dogma of Jesus' ministry with the later development of ecclesiastical confessions. It becomes apparent, also, if the actual development of the history of dogma is viewed from its beginnings to the present. In our century there is considerable skepticism concerning such continuity. The reason for this point of view is to be found in the past century, in the work of Ferdinand Christian Baur, the founder of the Tübingen school of theology, who with the help of Hegel's philosophy of history evolved a universal system of the history of dogma. Even though this system contained a very fascinating element, it was bound to stand or fall with Hegelian philosophy. According to Baur the history of dogma is a continual interaction (Prozessieren) of the Spirit with itself. Through thesis, antithesis, and synthesis the Spirit becomes aware of itself and, concurrently, reveals its true being, so that the germinal elements present in Christianity from the very beginning are gradually elevated to consciousness. This concept of history, which takes its position as it were from a point outside the world, has been strongly attacked, and rightly so. It is, in fact, much too one-sided to make possible an understanding of the many reasons and motives which have been of significance in the history of dogma. In our day, however, the opposite extreme would seem to be represented in the widespread tendency to see in particular dogmas only signs pointing toward something called "dogma," which is then vaguely characterized as the agreement of the church's proclamation with the revelation recorded in Scripture. For Barth and some of his followers the history of dogma is, ultimately, nothing but a succession of discrete signs pointing to the truth of revelation but bearing little or no relation to one another. It is not clear in Barth to what extent continuity in the history of dogma is possible, since for him dogmas are merely the forms in which "dogma" appears.

Still it seems possible that an unbiased observer can become convinced of the continuity of dogmatic development without having to think Hegelian thoughts. It is hardly an accident that the first dogma to be defined by the Christian church was the doctrine of the Trinity, with special emphasis being placed upon the relationship between Son and Father, and that the development of Christology followed thereafter with the definition, at Chalcedon, of the dogma of the two natures of Christ. Nor was it an accident that at approximately the same time the doctrine of sin and grace was clarified in the West, or that during the Middle Ages the doctrine of the sacraments was further developed, and that at the time of the Reformation the question concerning the appropriation of salvation became the central problem, one which led to the splintering of western Christianity and was then solved differently by Roman Catholics and Protestants. Nor is it an accident that in our day the question of the unity of the church is seemingly moving increasingly to the fore, so that perhaps the next steps in the development of the history of doctrine are to be expected in this area. At no time were the questions that called for dogmatic clarification questions of minor importance.

All dogmas, on the contrary, have to do with central problems which are of fundamental importance, both for the self-understanding of faith and for the content of faith. Dogmas and confessions, therefore, are a kind of catechism of the most important Christian truths.

If all this is kept in mind, it becomes difficult to deny that the history of dogma follows an autonomous trend in spite of the manifold motives and influences at work in it. If that is so then one should not dissolve the history of dogma into a series of confessions which are understood as isolated acts. The continuity in their development must always be kept in mind; in saying this, we are not attempting to support a traditionalism which simply clings to what is past and, as a result, forgets the tasks of the present. Attention must be paid both to the continuity of past development and to the actuality of contemporary questions and tasks.

SOURCE: Bernhard Lohse, *A Short History of Christian Doctrine* (Philadelphia: Fortress Press, 1966), pp. 8–12

4
Christian Uniqueness
Huston Smith

What is unique about Christianity in comparison with other religions? We wish to point out two hallmark elements: Christocentrism and emphasis on love. Christianity centers around a very particular person, Jesus the Christ, and it emphasizes the virtue of a joyful and unconditional love, triggered by encounter with the person of Jesus.

Monotheistic Christianity is substantially different from monotheistic Islam and Judaism in that Christianity is based on an incarnated monotheism: God is present in and through the very flesh of Jesus. Unlike the mythical gods of Greek and Roman polytheism, Jesus is historical: a person whose birth and life and death were bounded by the observable limits of time and space. Jesus reveals that the Christian God is personal, unlike the impersonal principle Brahman within some forms of Hinduism. Through Jesus the person, the radical separation between God and human beings is bridged; yet, unlike monism or a radical mysticism as in some branches of Buddhism, God and human persons are distinct, maintain their own individuality. Jesus the person also reveals that the God of Christianity is concerned about human beings, and that concern is exercised in human history and in the material world. Salvation, in light of the incarnation, is the freedom to be a human person and to relate lovingly with other human persons. Jesus the historical person reveals all of this.

Thus the Gospels point not to a system (as does Marxism) or to an ethical code (as does Confucianism) but to a person, Jesus the Christ, who is his very teaching. As guide and norm, Jesus reduces all commandments to the commandment of love (Mt. 22:34–40). Understood from Jesus' teaching and from his life, loving is not simply one virtue among others; it is the basic criterion of all virtues, of all principles, and of all forms of human behavior. This love is not simply a passive sentimentality but a demanding discipline as described by St. Paul (1 Cor. 13). Christian love is both an attitude and action of good will directed toward all, most especially toward those in need and near to us, as exemplified in the parable of the Good Samaritan. In sum, Christianity tells us that our relationship with God is impossible without a loving relationship with other human persons.

In our next selection, Huston Smith elaborates on Christocentrism and Christian love as the distinctive characteristics of Christianity and of Christians. Huston Smith was born in Soochow, China where he attended the Shanghai American School; he earned his Ph.D. at the University of Chicago. Smith has taught at a number of American universities; presently he is professor of religion and adjunct professor of philosophy at Syracuse University. His book *The Religions of Man,* from which the following excerpt is taken, has sold over two million copies and continues to be one of the most popular books on college campuses.

No one can doubt that ... [the] spirit [of Jesus] jumped dramatically to life, transforming a dozen or so disconsolate followers of a slain and discredited leader into one of the most creative groups in human history. We read that tongues of fire descended upon them. It was a fire destined to set the whole Mediterranean world aflame. Men who were not speakers became passionately eloquent. They exploded across the Graeco-Roman world, preaching what has come to be called the Gospel, but which, if translated literally, would be called the Good News. Starting in an upper room in Jerusalem, they spread their message with such ardor that in the very generation in which Jesus lived, it took root in all the leading cities of the region.

And what was this Good News that snapped Western history like a dry twig into B.C. and A.D. and left its impact through the Christian Church? Was it Jesus' ethical teachings—the Golden Rule, the Sermon on the Mount? Not at all. There is no teaching of Jesus that could not already be found in other literature of his day. Paul, whose letters epitomize the concerns of the early church knew a great deal about what Jesus had taught, but he almost never quotes him. Obviously the news he found so exciting was neither Jesus' ethical precepts nor even the phenomenal way in which his life had ex-emplified them. It was something quite different.

What this other something was may be approached through a symbol. If we had been living around the eastern Mediterranean in the early centuries of the Christian era we might have noticed scratched here and there on the sides of walls and houses or simply on the ground the crude outlines of a fish. Even if we had seen it in several places we would probably have dismissed it as a doodle—these were mainly seaport towns where fishing entered naturally into the lives of the people. If we had been Christians, however, we would have seen these fish as symbols of the Good News; their heads would have pointed us toward the place where the local Christian group held its underground meetings. For in those years of catacombs and arenas, when to be known as a Christian meant that one might be thrown to the lions or made into a human torch, Christians were forced to more cryptic symbols than the cross. The fish was one of their favorites, for the Greek letters for the word fish are also the first letters of the words "Jesus Christ, Son of God, Savior." This was the Good News, epitomized in the crude outline of an ordinary fish.

But what does the phrase itself mean: Jesus Christ, Son of God, Savior? Those who have grown up with it every Sunday may know the answer well. Our task, however, is to go behind the immense history of this phrase and try to work our way into what it meant to the men and women who first uttered it, for the entire subsequent history of Christianity grew out of their understanding of its significance.

In doing so one is tempted to plunge at once into ideas, defini-tions, and theology, but it will be wise to begin otherwise. Ideas are important in life, but they seldom, of themselves, provide starting points. They grow out of facts and experiences, and torn from this soil lose their life as quickly as uprooted trees. We shall find our-selves quite incapable of understanding Christian theology unless we manage to see clearly the experience it tried to account for.

The man in the street who first heard Jesus' disciples proclaim-ing the Good News was as impressed by what he saw as by what he heard. He saw lives that had been transformed—men and women or-dinary in every way except for the fact that they seemed to have found the secret of living. They evidenced a tranquility, simplicity, and cheerfulness that their hearers had nowhere else encountered. Here were people who seemed to be making a success of the greatest enterprise of all, the enterprise of life itself.

Specifically there seemed to be two qualities in which their lives abounded. The first of these was mutual affection. One of the earliest observations about Christians we have by an outsider was, "See how these Christians love one another." Here were men and women who not only said that all men were equal in the sight of God but who lived as though they believed it. The conventional barriers of race and status meant nothing to them. For in Christ there was neither Jew nor Gentile, Greek nor barbarian, bond nor free. As a consequence, in spite of differences in function or social position, their fellowship was marked by a sense of real equality.

Just before his crucifixion Jesus told his disciples, "My joy I leave with you." This joy was the second quality that pervaded the lives of the early Christians. Outsiders found this baffling. These scattered Christians were not numerous. They were not wealthy or powerful. If anything, they faced more adversity than the average man or woman. Yet in the midst of their trials they had laid hold of an inner peace that found expression in a joy that was almost boisterous.

Perhaps radiant would be the more exact word, though Paul himself describes the Holy Spirit as intoxicating. Radiance is hardly the word we would use to characterize the average religious life, but none other fits so well the life of these early Christians. Paul is an example. Here was a man who had been ridiculed, driven from town to town, shipwrecked, imprisoned, flogged until his back was covered with stripes. Yet here was a life whose constant refrain was joy: "Joy unspeakable and full of glory." "Thanks be to God who giveth us the victory." "In all things we are more than conquerors." "God who commanded the light to shine out of darkness has shined in our hearts." "Thanks be to God for his unspeakable gift." The joy of these early Christians was unspeakable. As the Fifth Chapter of Ephesians suggests, they sang not out of convention but from the irrepressible overflow of their direct experience. Life for them had ceased to be a problem to be solved and had become a glory discerned.

What produced this love and joy in these early Christians? The qualities themselves are universally coveted—the secret is how they are to be had. The explanation, insofar as we are able to gather it from the New Testament record, is that three intolerable burdens had suddenly and dramatically been lifted from their shoulders. The first of these was fear, even the fear of death. We have the word of Carl Jung that he has yet to meet a patient over forty whose problems did not root back to fear of his approaching death. The reason the Christians could not be intimidated by the lions and even sang as they entered the arena was that this fear had lost its hold. "Grave, where is thy sting?"

The second burden from which they had been released was guilt. Some persons contend that it is difficult for contemporary man to understand the ancients on this score because they assume guilt to be a vanishing phenomenon. Psychologists do not agree. They see modern man as weighted down by enormous guilt feelings. Indeed, it seems impossible for man to by-pass guilt feeling. No one can live without drawing distinctions of some sort between what he judges to be better and worse. Out of these distinctions there arises in every life a concept of what that life might be. Paralleling this, inevitably, runs the sense of failure. The times that we violate our norms are not confined to ones in which we treat other people less well than we should; they include opportunities for ourselves that we let slip irretrievably. . . . Unrelieved guilt always reduces creativity. In its acute form it can rise to a fury of self-condemnation that stifles creativeness completely and brings life to a standstill. Paul had felt its force before he gained his personal release: "Wretched man that I am, who will deliver me from this body of death?" (Rom. 7:24).

The third release the Christians experienced was from the cramping confines of the ego. There is no reason to suppose that prior to their new life these men and women had been any more self-centered than the next person, but this was enough for them to know that their love was radically infected with failure. They knew, in the words of a contemporary poet, that "the human curse is to love and sometimes to love well, but never well enough." Now this curse had been dramatically lifted. In Paul's "I live, yet not I, but Christ liveth in me," the circle of self was broken leaving love to flow freely from its former, self-demanding constraints.

It is not difficult to see how release from guilt, fear, and self could give men a new birth into life. If someone were actually to save us from these devastating drags against our love and joy, we too would call him savior. But this only pushes our question back a step. How did the Christians get free of these burdens? And what did a man named Jesus, now gone, have to do with the process that they should credit it as his achievement?

The only power that can effect transformations of the order we have described is love. It remained for our generation to discover that locked within the atom is the energy of the sun itself. For this energy to be released, however, the atom must be bombarded from without. So too there is, locked within every human life, a wealth of love and joy that partakes of God himself, but it too can be released only through external bombardment, in this case the bombardment of love. We see this clearly in child psychology. No amount of threat or preachment will take the place of the parents' love in nurturing a loving and creative child. We are beginning to see the point likewise in psychotherapy where love is coming to be a key term in theories of treatment.

This love of God is precisely what the first Christians did feel. They became convinced that Jesus was God and they felt directly the force of his love. Once it reached them it could not be stopped. Melting the barriers of fear, guilt, and self, it poured through them as if they were sluice gates, expanding the love they had hitherto felt for others until the difference in degree became a difference in kind and a new quality which the world has come to call Christian love was born. Conventional love is evoked by lovable qualities in the beloved—beauty, gaiety, friendliness, cheerfulness, personal charm, or some other. The love men encountered in Christ needed no such virtues to release it. It embraced sinners and outcasts, Samaritans and enemies; it gave not prudentially in order to receive, but because giving was its nature. Paul's famous description of Christian love in the Thirteenth Chapter of First Corinthians ought never ... to be read as if he were making a few supplementary observations about a "love" with which we are already familiar. It defines by indication, pointing not to something generally experienced by all men everywhere, like greenness or warmth, but to Jesus Christ. In phrases of classic beauty it describes the divine love which the Christian, insofar as he feels himself encompassed by the love of God, will reflect toward others. The reader should approach this chapter as if he were encountering the definition of some new conception, a quality which, as it had appeared "in the flesh" only in Christ, Paul was describing for the first time.

> Love is patient and kind; love is not jealous or boastful; it is not arrogant or rude. Love does not insist on its way; it is not irritable or resentful; it does not rejoice at wrong, but rejoices in the right. Love bears all things, believes all things, hopes all things; endures all things. Love never ends. ... (1 Cor. 13:4–8).

So astonishing did the first Christians find this love and the fact that it had actually entered their lives that they had to appeal for help in describing it. Paul, in closing one of the earliest recorded sermons on the Good News, turned back to the words of one of the prophets who in turn was speaking for God: "Look at this, you scornful souls, and lose yourselves in wonder, for in your days I do such a deed that, if men were to tell you this story, you would not believe it."

SOURCE: Huston Smith, *The Religions of Man* (New York: Perennial Library, 1965), pp. 313–319.

II
Jesus:
An Ideally Related Person

Introduction

Christianity is not *essentially* a philosophical-moral system that gives a blueprint for just living. It may have that effect on some of its adherents, but that is not its essence. Rather, Christianity is essentially an attachment to a person, an historical person, a Jewish person, a divine person, Jesus of Nazareth.

John Henry Newman, the great British Christian and practical philosopher of the nineteenth century, observed that attachment to persons is a far more potent force for living than attachment to speculative conclusions. He once remarked that he didn't know anyone who would die for a conclusion, but he knew thousands who would give their lives for another individual.

> The heart is commonly reached, not through reason, but ... by means of direct impressions, by the testimony of facts and events, by history, by description. Persons influence us, voices melt us, looks subdue us, deeds inflame us.... No man will be a martyr for a conclusion.... No one, I say, will die for his own calculations; he dies for realities (J. H. Newman, *Discussions and Arguments,* Longmans, Green and Co., London, 1885, p. 293).

By contrast, many other ways of life (and religions) draw their strength primarily from the *ideas* of their founders, from the preached message of their founders. A Freudian psychologist would not be shattered if he discovered that Freud did not execute well the counseling principles he formulated. A Marxist would probably not change his theories if he discovered that Karl Marx owned some private property. In these instances, the principles and ideas of the founders can be true in themselves, simply because they fit reality, regardless of the life-style of the founder.

Even a Muslim's or a Confucianist's convictions would not be absolutely negated if Muhammad and Confucius did not exemplify their teachings. They would hope that it would be so; it would be ideal if it were so; it would add great credibility if it were so—but it is not absolutely necessary.

In Christianity, Jesus *is* his message. His person is his teachings. He claimed to be the genuine reflection of God the Father: "Have I been with you all this time, Philip, and you still do not know me? To have seen me is to have seen the Father" (Jn. 14:9). He claimed *to be* the "way, the truth and the life"; he did not merely claim to preach and explain them.

It is the thesis of this book that, if one carefully studies the person and life of Jesus, one will discover that he is an ideal expression of the four basic relationships that make up the totality of each human being's life: relationship to the Other, to the material world, to others, and to self.

Since Jesus is divine, since he is the reflection of the revealing God, the way in which he ideally expresses the four relationships may not be exactly what a psychologist would predict or a sociological survey would conclude. Jesus is mystery. He is an excellent example of that old truism, "God's ways are not always our ways." He forgives perfectly even when people contradict his most basic message (as at the crucifixion, "Father, forgive them for they know not what they do"). He associates with public sinners and adulteresses, and even allows them to embrace him in public! He gives a command about "turning the other cheek" which to this day we Christians still find a baffling mystery.

His person, therefore, as the model of the four basic relationships, may not always be logically explainable, immediately rational. His relationships with others may sometimes baffle human wisdom, perhaps even seem to contradict it. The person of Jesus dares to teach humankind some divine mysteries about human living. He teaches us how "to do the impossible."

The selections in this section will give a basic and general description of the person of Jesus. The articles in the following four sections will spell out, in some detail, the nature of each of the four basic relationships and how Christians should act within the relationships as they follow the person of Jesus.

5
Jesus as True Lord
John A. T. Robinson

Christians have boldly affirmed, since the prayer forumlaries of the second century, that Jesus of Nazareth is God. All the major Protestant, Catholic, Orthodox and Anglican churches affirm this today. It is no longer a theological problem, therefore, to determine whether or not Jesus can be called God. The first four ecumenical councils, Nicea (325), Constantinople (381), Ephesus (431), and Chalcedon (451), quite clearly state and restate this revealed truth. However, as the following selection will point out, the dogmatic definitions of these councils simply express the mystery. It is quite a mystery to believe that a first-century Jewish male is *the* Divine Being, the Lord of the universe, the One without beginning and without end. What is problematic are the issues flowing from this bold doctrine: How is Jesus God? What was Jesus like because he was God? Is anyone else Divine in the same sense that Jesus was? What does the fact of his being God do to his humanness?

John A. T. Robinson, the Anglican bishop of Woolwich, England and a New Testament scholar, "takes a crack" at answering some of these intricate questions in the following selection from his much acclaimed and highly controversial work, *Honest to God.* This book was regarded by many to be the herald of the "death-of-God" theology of the 1960's. It was purposely intended by its author to be a catalyst for discussion and re-evaluation in a rather cut-and-dry area of Christian belief. It is a "suggestive" bit of theologizing rather than a conclusive treatise. Robinson was highly responsible for stirring up the waters for two decades, while himself contributing some valuable insights into the problem areas.

His primary negative observation about traditional theology of Christ as God is that we have made it sound as though the Second Person of the Trinity was just "pretending" to be human. Christ came into the human condition and looked just like one of us, much as a prince in disguise among the poorest of his subjects. When his mission was accomplished, he threw off his disguise, ended his pretense and—there he was, God among us!

That's a provocative and, we would judge, a fair critique. Traditional theology does make it at least sound that way, if not actually stating on occasion: "That's the way it was." How many times have we heard teachers of Christianity pass off certain difficult passages in the Scriptures with: "Well, Jesus was just saying that according to his human nature, but in his divine nature he really knew everything that would happen"? Robinson entreats his colleagues to search for more accurate ways of speaking about the mystery of the God-man, for, after all, even the traditional councils state that God became a real human being, not that he pretended to be one.

The Anglican bishop's strongest positive suggestion for clarifying our theology of the divinity of Christ centers around the interpretation of the first verse in the first chapter of John's gospel. Instead of rendering it, "And the Word was God," he suggests that it is more faithful to the original Greek to translate it, "And what God was, the Word was." Hence, if we look at Jesus, we see everything that God is. Jesus is the window into God at work.

Some modern theologians criticize Robinson's approach for making Jesus less than the Father, for making him "too human." We don't agree. Robinson emphasizes what has been lacking in our theology of Christ's divinity and gives a fresh perspective to the problems involved in the mystery of the God-man.

The doctrine of the Incarnation and Divinity of Christ is on any count central to the entire Christian message and crucial therefore, for any reinterpretation is likely to be at its maximum and where orthodoxy has its heaviest investment in traditional categories. This is true both at the level of technical theology, where any restatement must run the gauntlet of the Chalcedonian Definition and the Athanasian Creed, and at the popular level, where one will quickly be accused of destroying the Christmas story. But if it is necessary in our thinking about God to move to a position 'beyond naturalism and supranaturalism', this is no less important in our thinking about Christ. Otherwise we shall be shut up, as we have been hitherto, to an increasingly sterile choice between the two.

Traditional Christology has worked with a frankly supranaturalist scheme. Popular religion has expressed this mythologically, professional theology metaphysically. For this way of thinking, the Incarnation means that God the Son came down to earth, and was born, lived and died within this world as a man. From 'out there' there graciously entered into the human scene one who was not 'of it' and yet who lived genuinely and completely within it. As the God-man, he united in his person the supernatural and the natural: and the problem of Christology so stated is how Jesus can be fully man, and yet genuinely one person.

The orthodox 'answer' to this problem, as formulated in the Definition of Chalcedon, is within its own terms unexceptionable—except that properly speaking it is not a solution but a statement of the problem. But as a correct statement, as 'a signpost against all heresies', it had—and has—an irreplaceable value. 'The Christological dogma saved the Church', says Tillich, 'but with very inadequate conceptual tools'. To use an analogy, if one had to present doctrine of the person of Christ as a union of oil and water, then it made the best possible attempt to do so. Or rather it made the only possible attempt, which was to insist against all efforts to 'confuse the substance' that there were two distinct natures and against all temptation to break the unity that there was but one indivisible person. It is not surprising, however, that in popular Christianity the oil and water separated, and the one or the other came to the top.

In fact, popular supranaturalistic Christology has always been dominantly docetic. That is to say, Christ only appeared to be a man or looked like a man: 'underneath' he was God. . . .

But even if such a view would be indignantly repudiated by orthodox Churchmen, and however much they would insist that Jesus was 'perfect man' as well as 'perfect God', still the traditional supranaturalistic way of describing the Incarnation almost inevitably suggests that Jesus was really God almighty walking about on earth, dressed up as a man. Jesus was not a man born and bred—he was God for a limited period taking part in a charade. He looked like a man, he talked like a man, he felt like a man, but underneath he was God dressed up—like Father Christmas. However guardedly it may be stated, the traditional view leaves the impression that God took a space-trip and arrived on this planet in the form of a man. Jesus was not really one of us; but through the miracle of the Virgin Birth he contrived to be born so as to appear one of us. Really he came from outside.

I am aware that this is a parody, and probably an offensive one, but I think it is perilously near the truth of what most people—and I would include myself—have been brought up to believe at Christmas time. Indeed, the very word 'incarnation' (which, of course, is not a Biblical term) almost inevitably suggests it. It conjures up the idea of a divine substance being plunged in flesh and coated with it like chocolate or silver plating. And if this is a crude picture, substitute for it that of the Christmas collect, which speaks of the Son of God 'taking our nature upon him', or that of Wesley's Christmas hymn, with its 'veiled in flesh the Godhead see'.

But my point is not to ask how far particular expressions, or the general trend of thought they present, verge on the limits of orthodoxy but to put the question whether the entire supranaturalistic frame of reference does not make anything but a Christological tour de force impossible. For as long as God and man are thought of as two 'beings', each with distinct natures, one from 'the other side' and one from 'this side', then it is impossible to create out of them more than a God-man, a divine visitant from 'out there' who chooses in every respect to live like the natives. The supranaturalist view of the Incarnation can never really rid itself of the idea of the prince who appears in the guise of a beggar. However genuinely destitute the beggar may be, he is a prince; and that in the end is what matters.

But suppose the whole notion of 'a God' who 'visits' the earth in the person of 'his Son' is as mythical as the prince in the fairy story? Suppose there is no realm 'out there' from which the 'Man from heaven' arrives? Suppose the Christmas myth (the invasion of 'this side' by 'the other side')—as opposed to the Christmas history (the birth of the man Jesus of Nazareth—has to go? Are we prepared for that? Or are we to cling here to this last vestige of the mythological or metaphysical world-view as the only garb in which to clothe story with power to touch the imagination? Cannot perhaps the supranaturalist scheme survive at least as part of the 'magic' of Christmas?

Yes, indeed, it can survive—as myth. For myth has its perfectly legitimate, and indeed profoundly important, place. The myth is there to indicate the significance of the events, the divine depth of the history. . . .

The New Testament says that Jesus was the Word of God, it says that God was in Christ, it says that Jesus is the Son of God; but it does not say that Jesus was God, simply like that.

What it does say is defined as succinctly and accurately as it can be in the opening verse of St. John's Gospel. But we have to be equally careful about the translation. The Greek runs: *kai theos en ho logos*. The so-called Authorized Version has: 'And the Word was God.' This would indeed suggest the view that 'Jesus' and 'God' were identical and interchangeable. But in Greek this would most naturally be represented by 'God' with the article, not *theos* but *ho theos*. But, equally, St. John is not saying that Jesus is a 'divine' man, in the sense with which the ancient world was familiar or in the sense in which the Liberals spoke of him. That would be *theios*. The Greek expression steers carefully between the two. It is impossible to represent it in a single English word, but the New English Bible, I believe, gets the sense pretty exactly with its rendering, 'And what God was, the Word was'. In other words, if one looked at Jesus, one saw God—for 'he who has seen me, has seen the Father'. He was the complete expression, the Word, of God. Through him, as through no one else, God spoke and God acted: when one met him one was met—and saved and judged—by God. And it was to this conviction that the Apostles bore their witness. In this man, in his life, death and resurrection they had experienced God at work; and in the language of their day they confessed, like the centurion at the Cross, 'Truly this man was the Son of God'! Here was more than just a man: here was a window into God at work. For 'God was in Christ reconciling the world to himself'. . . .

And thus it comes about that it is only on the Cross that Jesus can be the bearer of the final revelation and the embodiment of God's decisive act: it is 'Christ crucified' who is 'the power of God and the wisdom of God'. For it is in this ultimate surrender of self, in love 'to the utter-most', that Jesus is so completely united to the Ground of his being that he can say, 'I and the Father are one. . . . The Father is in me and I am in the Father'.

It is in Jesus, and Jesus alone, that there is nothing of self to be seen, but solely the ultimate, unconditional love of God. It is as he emptied himself utterly of himself that he became the carrier of 'the name which is above every name', the revealer of the Father's glory—for that name and that glory is simply Love. The 'kenotic' theory of Christology, based on this conception of self-emptying, is, I am persuaded, the only one that offers much hope of relating at all satisfactorily the divine and the human in Christ. Yet the fatal weakness of this theory as it is stated in supranaturalist terms is that it represents Christ as stripping himself precisely of those attributes of transcendence which make him the revelation of God. The underlying assumption is that it is his omnipotence, his omniscience, and all that makes him 'superhuman', that must be shed in order for him to become truly man. On the contrary, it is as he empties himself not of his Godhead but of himself, of any desire to focus attention on himself, of any craving to be 'on an equality with God', that he reveals God. For it is in making himself nothing, in his utter self-surrender to others in love, that he discloses and lays bare the Ground of man's being as Love. . . .

SOURCE: John A. T. Robinson, *Honest To God* (Philadelphia: Westminster Press, 1963), pp. 64–68, 70–71, 73, 74–75.

6
Jesus as Truly Human
Harvey Cox

During much of Christian history, the divinity of Jesus has been emphasized. Perhaps that is why our following selection will make some of our readers uncomfortable. Its author, Harvey Cox, is attempting to better understand the humanity of Jesus.

Jesus was human. He was born with a heritage, a race, and a nation. He acquired a language and a religion. He grew up in a family context, worked in a carpenter shop, attended synagogue and temple services, joined in wedding festivities, and paid taxes to Caesar. Jesus was not a twentieth-century man but a Jew of first-century Israel.

No doubt, Jesus sweated and experienced thirst as he walked over that rough and craggy land on the eastern Mediterranean, a land then under the strong grip of the Roman legions. He rubbed elbows with peasants and with shepherds who were still numerous among a people whose ancestors were nomads. Jesus selected many of his disciples from among the early and rugged fishermen of Galilee, relatively prosperous men who owned boats and had access to the rich fisheries of the Lake of Galilee. Traders, merchants and the professional classes made their homes in the few sizable cities of Israel like Jerusalem where Jesus visited, preached, and participated in Jewish religious services.

This was the land and the people the man Jesus knew. As a human person, Jesus was there, sharing his presence, his friendship, his example, his preaching about the kingdom and the will of the Father. He experienced suffering and joy; he had enemies and friends; he knew defeat and success. In one sense, Jesus the man was divine because he challenged himself and others to be fully human; for to be fully human is to be the image of God, or that which is most divine.

It must be emphasized that in the following excerpt Cox is in no way demeaning Jesus or denying the divinity of Jesus. Cox is, after all, a Baptist minister, theologian, sociologist, and professor at Harvard Divinity School. However, in this article, written for the Christmas edition of *Playboy* magazine, January 1970, Cox does maintain that the inability to understand Jesus as a man—of his own time, country, and people—distorts the reality of Jesus; and Cox points out that Christians have, indeed, distorted the humanity of Jesus by:

(a) wrongfully portraying Jesus as an ascetic and thereby turning Christianity into a dreary life-denying philosophy;

(b) wrongfully picturing Jesus as a finicky moralizer and thereby transforming Christianity into a petty-rule system;

(c) wrongfully deradicalizing Jesus and thereby establishing him and Christianity as the cornerstone of a status quo.

A decisive question for Christianity has always been: "Who is Jesus?" Answers have varied throughout history, as the New Testament itself points out. But that Jesus was "flesh and bones," a human person in many ways similar to each of us, there is no doubt.

A yuletide toast! Lift the brimming beaker to that much maligned and badly misunderstood figure in Christmas lore, Ebenezer Scrooge. A heavy too long in the hearthside morality tales, Ebenezer deserves an immediate rehabilitation, if only for one reason: His classic two-word description of Christmas is so elegant, so succinct and so true that saying anything more seems almost redundant. "Christmas? Bah, humbug!" . . .

Christmas *is* humbug in the precise dictionary sense; i.e., "a fraud or imposition, sham, trickery, deception or swindle." Christmas is all these things and more. Oh, I'm not denying there are some good things about it. The whole season exudes a funny magic that gets to almost everyone in some way. But this happens *despite* what we've done to Christmas, not because of it. Who is responsible for ruining Christmas? . . .

... The blame for despoiling Christmas lies not with the hucksters, however boorish they may be. Christmas was messed up before they ever got hold of it. ... It is the churches that must accept the main responsibility for the truth of Scrooge's apt epithet. ...

How have the churches mutilated Christianity and, in the process, reduced Christmas to humbug? In a number of ways:

1) They have tried to make the story of Jesus over into a legend about an eviscerated, bloodless ascetic and Christianity itself into a dreary life-denying philosophy of flesh-despising abstemiousness. Admittedly, this has often been a little hard to manage, in view of the Biblical portrait of Jesus. On at least two occasions, the Gospels report that his enemies rejected Jesus because he had no interest in fasting and was "a glutton and a wine-bibber." He frequented parties, kept company with notoriously shady characters and supplied some booze when an embarrassed wedding-reception host found he was running low. I wonder who drew those countless pictures distributed by churches and Sunday schools of a pale, effete Jesus? Those pictures have done more to destroy Jesus than 100 of Herod's legions.

Someday, theologians may even have the courage to speculate openly on an aspect of Jesus' life that, until now, has remained strictly *sub rosa:* his relationship to women. If Jesus was fully man as well as fully God (which is orthodox Christian doctrine), then how did Jesus the man relate to women? As far as I know, only one contemporary theologian, Tom Driver of Union Theological Seminary, has ever risked writing an article on this delicate, if not taboo, subject. The speculation has been left to writers such as D. H. Lawrence and playwrights such as the contemporary Belgian dramatist Michel de Gheldrode. Lawrence, in his story THE MAN WHO DIED, equates the Resurrection with the awakening in Jesus of sensual desire. This loads entirely too much symbolic significance on sex, but it does help somewhat by taking Jesus out of the eunuchs' union. Gheldrode, in his play THE WOMEN AT THE TOMB, has all the women Jesus met during his lifetime—Mary Magdalene, the woman taken in adultery, the woman at the well, Mary and Martha and others—gather in a shack near the site of the Crucifixion and jealously rail at one another about what he had meant to each of them. The sensual aspect of many of these relationships is made quite clear and, furthermore, seems very natural.

Of course, Lawrence and Gheldrode are merely guessing. The Bible itself says nothing about the sexual aspects of Jesus' relationships. But it also says nothing at all about what Jesus did between the ages of 12 and 30. So story-tellers rush in where theologians fear to tread. And the spirit of what they say may be closer to the truth than the embarrassed evasions of the theologians. In any case, Jesus explicitly rejected the way of the anchorite or the Fakir. He did not flee to the desert with John the Baptist (though he apparently toyed with the idea at one time) nor did he join the puritanical Essenes on the shores of the Dead Sea. Jesus was not an ascetic. And the centuries-old effort of clerics, especially celibate ones, to geld Jesus into a prissy androgyne is one of the reasons Christmas today is a bamboozle. Who wants to celebrate the birthday of a First Century Teetotaling Myra Breckinridge?

2) The churches have also helped to destroy Christmas by turning Christianity into a petty-rule system and picturing Jesus as a finicky moralizer who spent his life telling people what NOT to do. This clerical casting of Jesus as a harried cubmaster is an even worse violation of the record than dressing him in a hair shirt of an ascetic. Jesus came into a world in some ways like ours, where, for most people, religion had been reduced to a set of rigid rules to worry about and a bag of ritual flip-flops to break open when you transgressed them. Jesus himself spent his life breaking most of those taboos—violating the Sabbath, rapping with "impure" men and women, wandering around with no visible means of support, sharply ridiculing the righteous prudes of the day. When people did come with moral dilemmas, he invariably tossed the questions back at them at a deeper level. Whether he was confronted by what some considered to be theft, adultery, tax evasion or whatever, he consistently refused to play the rulebook game. That is just what riled so many people. He made them look within and decide for themselves. And that's scary.

This is not to say that Jesus had no interest in the great ethical issues of life. He certainly did. But there is a difference between genuine morality and petty moralism. Jesus was concerned about the folly of looking for real satisfaction in obsessively accumulating wealth. He fought ethnic hatred, religious snobbery, intellectual pretense and every form of cultural hauteur. But a purveyor of rules he was not. How, then, have the priests made him into one?

Simple. Most people don't like to assume the responsibility of making ethical decisions for themselves. They long desperately for someone, anyone, to do it for them: a shrink, a professor, Ann Landers. Jesus refused. He was crucified. But the churches have gladly obliged. So instead of a feast of freedom and a time for celebrating the gift of choice, the churches have turned Christmas into one more doleful reminder of how grievously we have all wandered astray and how badly we need to be set back on the straight path. Perhaps the most appropriate way to mark the birthday of Christ, in his spirit, would be to pick out a particularly offensive cultural taboo (not a sexual one; that's too easy) and celebrate Christmas by transgressing it. Maybe that would mean taking a street-walker to midnight mass or burning money on the steps of the First National Bank. Whatever it is, transgression is good for the soul. And it also might lower the humbug level of Christmas, if only by a cubit.

3) The ecclesiastical powers have also made Christmas into a flim-flam by deradicalizing Jesus. This is their most astonishing example of prestidigitation. After all, this man was executed by the Roman authorities (no, Lenny, your people didn't do it; we goyim did) because they considered him to be a *political* threat. No imperial power wastes nails, boards and soldiers' time crucifying contemplatives or harmless spiritual mystics. Jesus was neither. In fact, recent research by Professor S. G. F. Brandon, an English New Testament scholar, suggests that he was probably much closer to the Zealots (the Viet Cong of occupied Palestine) than has previously been thought, or at least admitted. That question remains an open one. In any case, the life and message of Jesus is ill suited as material for an establishment ideology. But the elders are truly wise, and also inventive. The real miracle of transubstantiation is not that the Church turns wine into blood, but that it has transformed Jesus into a cosmic Tory. The song Jesus' mother sings after she conceives him calls for "casting down the mighty from their thrones" and "sending the rich away empty." Jesus himself announced that his mission was one of liberating the captives. He lampooned the rich, scorned those in power and defied imperial authority. He cast his lot with the outs, the riffraff and the misfits, the Palestinian equivalent of hippies, street people and untouchables. He died the death reserved for those found guilty of insurrection. On the whole, an unlikely candidate for the Union League Club.

Christmas is a swindle because the churches have taken a Jesus who was the hope of beleaguered underdogs and made him the keystone of the *status quo.* Although an occasional Christian today catches a glimpse of the revolutionary portent of Jesus, the churches usually do all they can to discourage such impiety. Camilo Torres, the guerilla priest of Colombia, and Eduardo Mondlane, the leader of the Mozambique National Liberation Front, both modern Christian rebels, are dead now, the victims of political assassination. But before they were murdered, they were already being pilloried by their fellow Christians for not showing patience under tribulation. You rarely see their pictures in churches or read about them in religious literature.

The con game continues. And until the churches forego their hard-won seats in the halls of the establishment and loose the radical potential in Christianity, the vast majority of the world's restive and enraged poor will rightly continue to see Christmas not only as humbug but as fir-scented opiate for the masses who are less and less willing to be drugged.

So there you have it. Christmas is a shell and the blame lies, for the most part, on those of us who call ourselves Christians. Why has it happened? Every religion has at least two sides, and Christianity is no exception. The figure of Christ has inspired Mozart's Requiem Mass, John Hus' rebellion, Giotto's painting and an endless succession of great men. Christianity has also been used as a knout for social control, a whip to punish and impoverish. There seem to be two Christs locked in combat. The clerical Christ, the one defined by ecclesiastical authority, is usually, though not always, the oppressive one. On the other hand, the most moving and authentic depictions of Christ often come from those on the edge or completely outside ecclesiastical Christianity. Thus, in our time, the most original filmic portrayal of Christ was made by an Italian Marxist and atheist, Pier Paolo Pasolini (*The Gospel According to St. Matthew*). The most vigorous modern retelling of Christ's life was written by Nikos Kazantaskis (*The Last Temptation of Christ*). But Kazantaskis was relentlessly attacked by the authorities of the Greek Orthodox Church and, when he died, was refused burial. The reason Christmas is humbug is that the churches are jealous and anxious. They want a monopoly on the portrayal of Christ and the definition of his significance. But they no longer have it, and that is all to the good. Jesus is not the churches' property. Christmas will continue to be humbug until the churches realize that fact and loose their death grip on him. . . .

So I lift my flagon to old Ebenezer. He tells it like it is. But as I drink, I secretly have another toast in mind, too, a toast to Christmas. Not the humbug Christmas we Christians have foisted on the world, admittedly with a little help from our friends at Gimbels and Saks. No, I drink Christmas as it may someday be: a fiesta when we celebrate earth and flesh and, in the midst of all our hang-ups and tyrannies, remind ourselves that at least once one guy lived a reckless, ecstatic and fully free life *every* day—and that maybe someday we all can.

SOURCE: Harvey Cox, "For Christ's Sake," *Playboy* Magazine 16 (January 1970), pp. 117, 122, 238–239.

III
Relationship with the Other

Introduction

Christianity affirms an interesting paradox that each of us instinctively knows about the nature of the human person: every human being is limited, but yearns to go beyond all limits. Every person experiences the boundaries of his or her existence, but is never satisfied to stay inside those boundaries.

Each time that a new scientific discovery is made, someone immediately predicts that it is "only the beginning" of a vast new area of the unexplored. Each time that an athletic record is broken (the four-minute mile was once regarded as unthinkable!), there is a supple young athlete waiting in the wings to break it once again. The towering masterpiece of present-day music will become an "old classic" fifty years from now, and a new genius will arrange the notes in a way that no past master ever dreamed of.

The paradox continues. The more that we as thinking persons strive to transcend our own limitations, the more we discover how incapable we are of doing it completely by ourselves. No matter how great the achievement, how startling the progress, it will always be "only another step" and temporary. The human person needs help from somewhere, but every other human source seems as limited as the "I" who is striving. Where can the yearner look for this fulfilling help? We may look only to the Other, to the unlimited, to transcendence, to the infinite—Christians call this God.

Jesus reveals what our own human natures experience, that we human persons need God in order to be fulfilled. "Without me you can do nothing." "With me all things are possible." Very simply, Christianity teaches that we just can't make it by ourselves.

There is yet another step in our paradox. If human beings yearn for the unlimited, if we come to know that we cannot achieve this by ourselves, no matter how hard we try, if we know that we *need* the transcendent, then what is there that limited persons can do to gain some help from the Other? The answer is simple. In a strict sense, there is nothing that a human being can do to assure contact with God. The human being can ask—even beg—that the transcendent will come if a person is obedient and just and virtuous. But, in the last analysis, we cannot "force the hand" of the Divine. The limited cannot control the Unlimited.

On the other hand, God has revealed that he is always in the act of giving the Divine Self to human beings. God is never far from us, never holding back. All we need do is open ourselves and allow the Divine Friend to pour into us. As a fish in a pond is surrounded by water, so we are deluged with Godness. It is not our doing that we are so surrounded; the Lord has taken the initiative. But we must open the floodgates and allow the Divine to drench us thoroughly.

This is the essence of Christian teaching concerning the relationship of God and human beings: God freely chooses to be in touch with men and women in order that they may fulfill their most basic created yearning; God has freely chosen to do so preeminently through Christ.

The selections in this section will treat of some of the highlights of this paradoxical relationship between the infinite God and his limited creatures.

7
Grace
Karl Rahner

Nothing has burdened the Catholic Christian theology of grace more than the popular concept that grace is a "thing," a "commodity," a "stuff," that can be measured like B.T.U.'s (British thermal units) in a physics lab. Catechists and preachers have enhanced this image by speaking constantly of "increases of grace," or of the "sacraments pouring grace into believers" like pipelines into a receptacle tank.

Grace is not a "thing," a measurable commodity. That's a most unfortunate metaphor. It speaks of a mechanical concept of salvation (pour enough in and one is saved!). Rather, grace is essentially a relationship between a human person and God. It is a bond of unity, a bond of friendship. The theology of grace tells of what happens when a human being comes into contact with God. It insists that a person cannot come into touch with God without being changed, and then attempts to describe the details of the change (e.g., a power to love everyone, an ability to see a divine dimension in all reality).

Such a changed person is called *holy* (an Old English word meaning "whole, sound, happy") because that person is totally available to God. The holy person is inspired to respond with outstanding faith, hope and love to the sociological, political and economic challenges of the time. Holiness is thus a manifestation of grace.

The outstanding genius of mid-twentieth-century Catholic theology, Karl Rahner, has written prolifically on the topic of grace. He has written on it creatively, yet with a great interest in being faithful to past Christian tradition. Professor of systematic theology at the University of Munich, he has had a special interest in the question of how the grace experience is related to created human nature. This is the topic of his work, *Nature and Grace,* from which the following selection has been taken.

Rahner's main point of emphasis here is that the yearning for a relationship with God is natural to a human being. It is not something superadded to us after we have gone around "being purely human" for a while. It is part of the very fibre of our beings, it is innate, it is a portion of the very definition of what it is to be human. That this yearning is within us by the very fact of our humanness is indicated, according to Rahner, by universal human experiences such as "discontent which cannot find rest, anguish at the insufficiency of material things, protest against death. . . ." Consequently, "supernatural destiny" does not mean a destiny that is not native to a human person; it means simply that it is beyond our power to achieve it on our own.

Rahner's conclusion is simple: there is no such reality as "pure nature" without a supernatural destiny. This paradox is at the heart of our theology of grace as a relationship, viz., the finite (human being) yearns for the infinite (God), and is not satisfied, not fulfilled, until it is attained. It is attained ("rendered to us by God" would be more accurate) in the grace relationship.

One final exhortation to the reader before you dive into this selection. Be aware that it is one of the more difficult readings in this anthology. We have chosen it because we feel that Rahner's brilliance should not be bypassed, even in a popular volume such as this. Read it patiently; read it expectantly with hopes for great insight when you capture his meaning. Remember the Jewish proverb from the Talmud as you read: "It is not the same to study a piece one hundred times as it is to study it one hundred and one times."

When a man is called by the message of faith of the visible Church, this call does not come to a man who is brought by it (and by his conceptual knowledge) for the first time into contact with the reality proclaimed; but it is a call which makes him reflect on and realize (and of course makes him take up a position towards) what was before the unrealized but truly existing grace present in him as an element of his spiritual existence. Preaching is the awakening and making explicit of what is already there in the depths of man, not by nature but by grace. Grace which enfolds man, the sinner and the unbeliever too, as his very sphere of existence which he can never escape from.

At this point we have now at last reached and can properly formulate the actual problem "nature and grace" in the narrower sense. It is clear that in the living of his mental and spiritual life man is aware of his "nature", even in the theological sense in which it is the opposite to grace and the supernatural. For when he reflects on himself, he experiences himself in every judgment of himself in which he looks at himself as an object and sees himself in his transcendence towards the infinite as something which cannot be dissolved into unknown quantities, and which exists as a whole or not at all; he grasps his metaphysical essence, spirit in transcendence and freedom. And from this transcendental analysis of what is said implicitly about man in every human act, he must then go on to see many other things as "essential" to man; his being in the world, his bodiliness, his belonging to a community of fellow men. In short, there is a metaphysical knowledge of man's essence, primarily here, of his nature, by the light of his reason, meaning independent of revelation; but also through a means (his reason) which is itself a part of the essence thus grasped. But for the theological reasons already given, it is also true that the actual human nature which is here experiencing itself need not, and cannot, regard all that it thus experiences as "pure" nature, as distinct from supernatural (particularly if this self-experience of man is seen in the context of the whole of human history, without which it cannot reach full awareness). Actual human nature is never "pure" nature, but nature in a supernatural order, which man (even the unbeliever and the sinner) can never escape from; nature superformed (which does not mean justified) by the supernatural saving grace offered to it. And these "existential facts" of his concrete (his "historical") nature are not just accidents of his being beyond his consciousness but make themselves apparent in his experience of himself. He cannot clearly distinguish them by simple reflection (by the light of natural reason) from the natural spirituality of his nature. But when once he knows through revelation that this order of grace exists, which is given to him unmerited and does not belong to his nature itself, then he will be more careful; he must take into account that perhaps many things which he concretely experiences in himself and ascribes almost involuntarily to his "nature" are in fact due to the working in him of what he knows from theology to be unmerited grace. Not as if he now no longer knew what was nature in him. The nature of spiritual being and its supernatural elevation are not like two things laid one beside the other, or one against the other, which must either be kept separate or the one exchanged for the other. The supernatural elevation of man is the absolute (although unmerited) fulfilment of a being which, because of its spirituality and transcendence towards infinite being, cannot be "defined", i.e., "confined", like sub-human beings. These are "defined" through its being of their very essence to be limited to a particular sphere of reality. (It would therefore be impossible, for example, for them to be "elevated" to a supernatural fulfilment; this elevation would take away their essence which essentially "confines" them.) The "definition" of the created spirit is its openness to infinite being; it is a creature because of its openness to the fullness of reality; it is a spirit because it is open to reality as such, infinite reality. So it is not surprising that the greatness of the fulfilment—the openness does not of itself require this absolute and unsurpassable fulfilment and has a meaning without it—cannot be immediately recognized as either "owing" or "unmerited". Nevertheless, in spite of the difficulty in distinguishing what is "nature" and what isn't, nature is not thereby overthrown. The beginnings of this fulfilment already exist—the experience of infinite longing, radical optimism, discontent which cannot find rest, anguish at the insufficiency of material things, protest against death, the experience of being the object of a love whose absoluteness and whose silence our mortality cannot bear, the experience of fundamental guilt with hope nevertheless remaining, etc. Because these beginnings are brought to absolute fulfilment by the power of God's grace, this means that in them we experience both grace and nature. For we experience our nature where we experience grace; grace is only experienced where by nature there is spirit. And vice versa; in fact, as things are, when spirit is experienced it is a supernaturally elevated spirit. As long as we keep these remarks about the relationship between nature and grace to the general and formal, no particular difficulty arises, although we are saying that we can only encounter nature as spirit in the supernatural order and never the spirit as "pure nature". But it becomes more difficult when we try to make precise statements on the concrete and individual level. What, precisely, in this nature is nature, and what would not be there but for its elevation to the supernatural order? For example, is the resurrection of the body part of man's natural destiny as a spiritual person, or does it only happen through grace? Or what would the final destiny of a pure nature be like in the concrete? These are questions which could only be answered if we could experiment with pure nature, and use our results as the basis of a theory of its final destiny. But as things are we cannot go beyond an essentially formal doctrine of a "natural" final destiny which—as from what has been said is naturally to be expected—is merely an abstract formalization of the concrete doctrine of a supernatural final destiny. This goes to show that medieval theology did well not to bother too much about a natural beatitude. Not only because there is in fact no such thing, but also because it is basically only the abstract formalization of the actual supernatural final destiny taught by theology (and not so very helpful), and because if an attempt is made to make it concrete, it is bound to borrow unjustifiably from theology.

SOURCE: Karl Rahner, *Nature and Grace* (New York: Sheed and Ward, 1963), pp 32–38.

8
Contemplation
William McNamara

Christians believe that God communicates with us in many ways: through Jesus, the Church, Scripture, nature, others, and even through our very selves. Nature reveals God's majesty and might; others reveal God's love and concern. Our own body and intellect and imagination reveal all this and more, for we are the image and likeness of God. In a very real sense, *I* am God's most basic communication—God's most basic word—to me. To journey into that word is to journey into the presence of God.

Prayer, meditation, and contemplation facilitate that journey into the presence of God by sensitizing and heightening our consciousness and thereby enabling us to experience the gifts of God's presence: moments of awe, strength and perseverance, contentment and peace. We have traditionally distinguished prayer, meditation and contemplation in Christian literature in the following way:

> —to pray is to offer petition, praise, and thanks to God;
> —to meditate is to reflect on the multitude of God's gifts;
> —to contemplate is simply to be in the presence of God.

All three, however are synonymous insofar as they enable us to be aware of God in our lives. Let us consider contemplation.

Contemplation is not a special privilege of monks. Contemplation is not an erudite technique used only by the masters of the spiritual life. Contemplation is not one of those rare experiences that come without warning, then vanish, never to return again.

No, contemplation is much simpler than all that. Contemplation is to come consciously into the presence of the living God in order to speak and to listen. One of the reasons why much of the popular Christian tradition seems to have associated contemplation with "special people" like monks and hermits and cloistered nuns is that we somehow got the idea that, to really find God, one had to "get away from it all." We seemed to presume that the more we removed ourselves from business and work, friendships and conversations, movies and plays, magazines and TV, the easier it would be to find God. This implies that God isn't within friendships and conversations, business and work, etc.

It is to this point that William McNamara addresses himself most strongly in his book *The Human Adventure* from which the following selection is taken. We Christians must not miss the fact that "the world is crammed with God" if we wish to lead full, human lives. God literally is in everything, is everywhere, is reflected in some way in all events. One does not find God by fleeing from reality; one finds the divine by plunging into reality, by taking "a long loving look at the real" (the title of the chapter in which this selection is to be found).

Most thinkers would agree that knowledge from experience is the most enduring, the most persuasive, the most valuable. To experience God means that we have discovered that he is in *this* cherry, *this* friend, *this* conversation, *this* dog. That's contemplation. We discover the divineness in any reality; we stop to look and wonder, speak and listen, and love.

Contemplation does not separate us from reality and make us "out of it." It cannot do that for, by very definition, contemplation is to be in touch with the foundation of reality, the heart of all reality, the one God. Our selection will conclude, therefore, that the contemplative (i.e., anyone who contemplates) can only be an earthy, compassionate, really real human being.

William McNamara's own life-style is an interesting commentary on this notion of contemplation. He spends

about six months each year out in the wilderness (either
in Arizona or Nova Scotia, at his "Spiritual Life Insti-
tutes"), wrapped in contemplation. He carefully explains
that he does not go out into the desert to "get away from
it all" but to get into it all. The other half of the year he
spends in a full schedule of teaching and preaching
throughout the United States. As you will glean from his
writing, he is convinced that any full schedule of work remains hollow, empty, frustrating unless one has had the
experience of Reality itself—challenging encounters with
the living God in contemplation.

The only way to know God is by experience: the way the lover
knows the beloved, the spouse knows the spouse, the friend knows
the friend, and the wise adventurer knows life. There is no other
way. We can get to know him in a hundred different ways. But the
only way to know him as he is in himself is by experience.

To experience something—anything—we need to enter into it in
a threefold way: by perceptive appreciation, participation, and interpretation.

By a perceptive appreciation of the thing itself: to perceive, to
recognize, to see things as they really are. To worship is to see the
real worth of things and respond to him who gives them their value.
To worship in spirit and truth is to catch the splendor and glory of
lilies and lions, of mud and men, not just the temple, and so to discover and respond to the presence of God everywhere, not just in
Jerusalem. To see that the world is crammed with God, that everything is a sign, a symbol, and a sample of him who summons us to be
and to contemplate: this is to imitate God who worked until the seventh day, then looked on what he created and found it all very good.

Looking directly at reality, affirming the intrinsic goodness of
things, coexperiencing with God the totality of being in a single
acorn or a blade of grass or an alley cat—that can be, and often is, a
high point of the human adventure. Wise men, Orientals especially,
are unimpressed by the trumpeted and truncated renewal going on in
the Western churches. They look with pity on our feverish activities,
our frantic rearrangement and reorganization of religious trumpery,
and ask so piquantly: But have you changed the inner eye? Without
this special kind of eyesight we shall never discover the inner splendor of things or their important connections.

The wise man is the experienced man who lives with his eyes
and his heart wide open, full of reverent wonder and radical amaze-

ment. But he is not equally open to everything. He perceives a hierarchy of being, a gradation of value. He discriminates, distinguishes, and discerns the spirit. He also recognizes and confronts the demonic dimensions of being, the mystery of iniquity. He knows that life is short and he is limited, so he sifts, selects, and chooses just that much of the raw material of this world that he knows he can infect with his love and transfigure with his spirit. He lives so wakefully and expectantly that little of value escapes his notice, and whatever is worthwhile evokes his loving attention. He sees the things of this world as rare treasures or as things never seen before.

Taking a long loving look at the cherry, delighting in its roundness and redness, is as important to him as eating it. Man does not live by bread alone—certainly not by the consumption of bread alone—but by the contemplation of bread. One hunger is satisfied by the consumption of a meal; a deeper hunger is satisfied by the contemplation of a meal. The perception of the social, aesthetic, and spiritual values involved, for instance, in the luscious sight and smell and taste of artichoke or avocado and the enjoyment of fine fellowship and good talk. When a husband ceases to take long loving looks at his wife, then no matter how much he copulates, his love diminishes and the marriage begins to fade. If I am pulled by multiple desires into the fancied future, I cannot see how much good fills the here and now. If I am driven by compulsion, I am not free to wait, to look around lovingly and longingly until I find what will not merely tease, taunt, and tantalize me sporadically, but will hold and captivate my focused attention and feed forever with prodigious prodigality the cold, passionate fury of my hunger. . . .

My brother recently chided me for wasting days and nights in fruitless prayer and search for a dog lost in the woods. "After all," he said, "it's just a dog, and you've got pressing things to do." I've got to make him understand there's no such thing as just a dog. Every dog expresses uniquely the dogginess of God, a quality of God that can be found nowhere else. God is that dog lost in the woods. While he is lost, though I may not and need not find him, there is no other way for me to seek God here and now except by seeking the lost dog. The search cannot be fruitless nor the time wasted. The dog, lost or found, cannot be loved too much. Love may be spoiled by mawkish sentimentality or egotistic instrusions, spoiled precisely because of the diminution of love; but love itself has no excess. . . .

A perceptive appreciation of things, which is the first indispensable element of experience, evokes reverence; and reverence is a key virtue; in fact, I think it is the keyest of all virtues. If I were delicately and distinctively reverent to myself, to others, to everything, to God, I would never sin. Sin is always an act of violence: twisting and distorting something or someone out of shape and out of harmony, and thus disrupting the universe, for my own private profit, pleasure, and purpose.

In addition to a perceptive appreciation, then, the second essential element of human experience is participation. It is not enough to see, to observe, to be a detached spectator. Life must be suffered. Experience is not the result of contrived "happenings" but the fruit of a man's total immersion in existence. He doesn't strive for neat little experiences. He simply spends himself, coping creatively with the exigencies, tragedies, and serendipities of the human adventure, suffering life with unconditional and unselfconscious abandon. It is imperative to recognize with Gabriel Marcel that life is not a series of problems to be solved but a mystery to be lived. Only by becoming a passionate participant in life can man enjoy a sense and knowledge of reality gained from direct intercourse and be led by this contact with the real into vital union with the ultimately Real, God himself. Exploration into God requires one kind of experience of every human being: the penetration of the real.

It is not enough to look at the woman; if we are to know her, we must dwell with her, share life with her. Pitying the poor man is not enough; we must share his poverty. Visiting the sick is a good deed half done; we must feel the pain. Mourning the death of a departed friend or relative is fitting; but we must also feel his presence more keenly now than before his death. "There but for the grace of God go I" is a kind gesture toward a criminal; but it would be more appropriate and compassionate to say and to feel: "There, hidden in that man's public crime, are all my private sins." People who announce preposterously that they don't like cats have never dwelt with a cat or been inundated with the feline quality of God. Hunters who kill deer for sport and raccoons for coats can't imagine what it is like to be a deer or a raccoon, or for that matter, what it is like to be the Creator of the deer and raccoon; or what it is like to be, as every man is, the custodian of God's creation, whose duty and privilege it is to take care of the universe. By that I mean: to help the universe realize goals that it cannot realize itself. W. H. Auden said: "I think we might have a decent world if it were universally recognized that to make a hideous lampshade, for example, is to torture helpless metals. And every time we make a nuclear weapon, we corrupt the morals of a host of innocent neutrons below the age of consent."

We tend only to have vicarious relationships with the real (book knowledge) and so deprive ourselves of the stuff of life as we move desultorily into a derivative existence. Some people, mostly young, have begun to break out of this dehumanized condition. But we have a long way to go. We need to get into the sun, the air, the water, the woods, the sand. We have to get into the squalor of the city with enough light and love to transfigure it. We have to get into the game and into the dance. Otherwise we will suffocate and die.

The third essential element of experience is interpretation. It unifies and integrates the multiple items of the experience, providing a processive pattern of meaning, a purpose, and an ultimate fruition. Interpreting the experience is like making a collage. It sees all the connections and possible relationships and gives a single focus and shape to a hundred different vibrations and relations. It achieves certainty, continuity, and integrity by directing human forces onward and upward, precluding the isolation and aberration of creative and imaginative human thrusts toward the transcendent.

The fruit of experience, the wholeness of life, requires good interpretation. A good football quarterback is a good interpreter. So is the live motorcyclist. He scans the field or the road, recognizes half a dozen problems at once, makes quick and appropriate judgments, moves deftly and adroitly, and he is in the clear. And so is a good man with a lively faith. He copes with the exigencies of life quickly, gracefully, and creatively. He is thus a moral man. Though he is thoroughly cognizant of the sudden, inextricable eruptions of a brand-new experience into the moral life of man that need to be freshly evaluated, he does not abandon in a panic or a rush of enthusiasm the permanent basic structure of morality. And whatever may be said about dynamic truths (the only kind that modern philosophers and theologians recognize), the good interpreter admits of static ones, too, in order to give a proper account of the reality we experience. He needs a conceptual scheme to describe the frame of reality needed for everyday discourse, and far more so, for our experience of the moral order. . . .

The only valid interpretation of my experience is myself. But no man is an island, so there is no such thing as an isolated human being. I am linked to all others and am irrevocably rooted in the Wholly Other. So my experience must be interpreted in terms of this intricately interlaced pattern of existence. I must ask: What does modern man have to say to the Church? And though I doubt he will have much more to say than he said so far, I must remain open to the possibility. A more enduringly important question is: What does the Church have to say to modern man?

I assume what the Church says to the world will be based on criteria of truth, not of sociocultural market research or public relations. I am not asking the modern Church, but the Church ever ancient and ever new. Its most recent message is essentially the same as its most ancient. The irrecusable wisdom of the ages is what is important. So I interpret my experience in the context of the long living tradition of the Church, not just the recent past, but the whole past alive in the present. The long view is a must. . . .

SOURCE: William McNamara, *The Human Adventure* (Garden City, N.Y.: Doubleday and Co., 1974), pp. 30–32, 34–36, 41–42.

9
Trust
Romano Guardini

Trust is the ability to let go. It is the willingness to place some of our destiny in the hands of another and be confident that the other person will care for that destiny well. In one sense, trust means that we willingly place ourselves at the mercy of another.

If trusting means "to let go," then trusting in self should mean that we are open to evaluating ourselves without any defense mechanisms. Trusting in self need not mean that "I can take care of everything by myself," that one doesn't really need anyone or anything else in order to live fully. It means rather that we are confident of our abilities and aware of our weaknesses. We are conscious of how far our own strength can take us and how much our limitations will need to be supported by faithful friends. For Christians, such an awareness leads us finally to rely on the only One who is perfectly self-sufficient, utterly faithful, always present—the one God.

The opposite of trust is "security," in the popular—and false—sense of the word. Security is popularly taken to mean that "I have it all sewed up," that nothing can go wrong because one has thought of everything ahead of time and double-checked to make sure that all is in order. In this bogus sense, security leads to a feeling of no need for others. Interaction with fellow human beings becomes a nicety rather than a necessity. Alienation rather than socialization is the result. A false sense of security tries to replace trusting; an authentic sense of security comes from trusting.

A striving for this popular kind of security alienates one, too, from a faithful God. It seems to say that any dependence on a Supreme Being is weakness and unfulfillment. It implies that the ideal person is the one who can get along without a God.

Romano Guardini, in the following selection on "Divine Providence," describes the experience of trusting in God as leading to human fulfillment. He wrestles with the mystery of how we can be free human beings and, at the same time, find a divine purpose in every reality and event. He doesn't solve that mystery. No human author ever will. However, one thing is certain in his theology. We are not puppets on a divine string, fitting into a prefabricated divine plan like interlocking pieces in a picture puzzle. There is no single, set, unbending divine scheme that is going to take place, no matter what free human beings do. Such a notion, frequently held on a popular level, is the worst kind of predestinationism. God is indeed present in every reality, can be discovered in every event, but that doesn't mean that he has determined the course of that event ahead of time and taken it completely out of human hands. We are free to shape reality—yet the divine is always there as we do. To trust, therefore, is simply to face the fact that God is present in order that free human beings may live without the anxiety that destroys the fullness of their experience.

Romano Guardini was professor of philosophy at the University of Munich, and before that a professor of the philosophy of religion at the University of Berlin. As a philosopher and speculative theologian, he has had a great interest in the problem, perhaps the paradox, of God's will and human freedom and has written widely on the issue.

The idea of Providence constantly recurs in the New Testament and expresses the essence of what Christ brought to man. A number of Christ's sayings refer to it: the one about the sparrow not falling from the roof without the Father's knowledge; about the birds He feeds and the flowers He clothes. We are exhorted not to worry about food and drink; to pray for bread today and tomorrow, entrusting the future to the Father's hands. Again and again, the mystery of Providence is expressed in the words "Your Father in heaven. . . ."

These sayings all imply that man's whole life and existence and everything that belongs to him is surrounded by an infinite goodness. Nothing that happens is purely accidental; the whole course of things is guided by a loving concern for man's welfare. We must not accept this too glibly. When we look around the world it does not seem that things really work out quite like that. Events go on their relentless way—and how often they ignore the individual and his happiness! Good men pine away and are unable to exert their influence to the full: they might have done so much good with their life-giving hands. Creative men die before they have borne their fruit; others prosper seemingly unjustly. The defenseless are violated. Pure thoughts can find no scope for expression; precious things are destroyed, but inferior, mediocre, vulgar things thrive and flourish. . . .

The world sometimes appears to be governed by senseless despotism and destructive chance. Sometimes it is as though a malicious spirit were at work destroying a thing of beauty just when it is on the point of blossoming, or a rare destiny the moment it is about to be fulfilled.

Someone may reply that nevertheless Order reigns supreme in the world, that everything is governed by exact laws. Certainly there is an Order in the world. But it is not concerned with man. It goes its way regardless of him. Or is it in fact designed to promote human fulfillment, or social justice, on however modest a scale? Perhaps we should say "individual fulfillment" rather than "human fulfillment" in general, since the human race consists of single individuals. Fulfillment can only mean that the individual's heart's desire is fulfilled, his creative urge given full scope, and his yearning for greatness consummated. But the universe ignores him: it goes its own way. The animals are not concerned with our affairs. They are caught up in the necessities of their own existence. The trees ignore us even when we eat their fruit. They grow and perish. The mountains do not look at us. They simply exist.

And yet people talk about "Providence."

What is Providence?

Providence would be if it were possible for me to be convinced that I, with my living personality, exist in an order which does not constrain me, as the atom is constrained by the natural law, which does not use me as the factory uses its workers, but is guided by my needs. Everything that happens would have me in mind. The course of the world would accord with the innermost needs of my nature. If we look at the world intelligently and on the basis of our experience the Order that governs it must seem cold and blind. "Providence" means, however, that there is a seeing Mind behind everything that happens and that I am the object of its seeing. It means that provision is being made for what is good for me. It means that there are eyes in the world which see everything, from which nothing is hidden that may injure or benefit me. It means that "not a hair of my head shall fall" without being noticed and assessed with regard to my welfare and salvation. It means that there is significance in everything that happens in the world, and a heart, a concern and a power stronger than all the powers of the world which is able to fulfill the purposes of its care for man.

It is not right to take the mystery of Providence too much for granted or to speak of it as a natural, slightly improbable, slightly sentimental order which governs the world. The idea of Providence is grounded on the whole audacity of a living faith. To believe in Providence, to realize the living faith in Providence, means to transform one's whole conception of the world. It ceases to be the world of natural science. It becomes alive. But it does not become a magic world in which strange things happen and which ceases to exist the moment we come to grips with stern reality. To believe in Providence it is not necessary to abstract the harshness from the world. The world remains what it is. Providence implies that the world, with its natural facts and necessities, is not enclosed in itself but lies in the hands of a Power and serves a Mind greater than itself. The laws of inert matter do not cease to apply once life takes hold of them any more than the laws of physical growth cease to apply when the human heart and mind are busy building up their world. They remain, but they serve a higher purpose. And once you discern this higher purpose you realize the service these forces and laws perform for it. Providence means that everything in the world retains its own nature and reality but serves a supreme purpose which transcends the world: the loving purpose of God.

But this love of God for His creatures whom He has made His children is alive like that of a human being for his dear ones. The love of a father for his child pursues him in all its developments, in all its fortunes, in all its ever-changing activities and decisions. So too the love of God for man is alive and ever new. And the whole world is drawn into the orbit of God's constant care for man. It embraces the whole world, past and present, in every passing moment of its existence and activity.

And so the world is renewed in every moment of time. Every moment has only one existence. It has not existed before and it will not come again. It springs from the eternity of God's love and takes all Being and all that is and all that happens into itself for the sake of God's children. Everything that happens comes to me from God, from His love. It calls me. It challenges me. It is His will that I should live and act and grow in it and become the person it is His will that I should be. And the world is to be perfected into that which it can become only through man—that is, through me.

But isn't all this just a beautiful story?

Or is it something I can only "believe" in the desperate sense of the word, without ever having a chance to experience it?

No, it is a reality, and it is possible to have personal experience of it.

There is a way of coming to experience it as a reality, and it is a way that is constantly recurring. It is "The Now."

It is possible to conceive the idea of Providence with the mind alone, purely theoretically, by arguing that God has created everything and that everything that happens fulfills His will. If the world appears to contradict this theory, it can be argued that the totality of the forces at work in the world is so varied and the texture of purposes so complex that we cannot penetrate it and that we can see through the tangle of human destinies still less and must console ourselves with the idea that what appears to be meaningless destruction may be serving an ultimate purpose. To believe this would be a great deal, but much more is possible.

Providence is a reality; and we must not merely conceive this reality theoretically: we must act upon it in our lives. It is not easy to express what I mean. A piece of news arrives: something has happened. The web of things and events and claims closes in around us. "It"—the situation . . . but no, it is not an "It" at all—at the deepest level of our minds we know it is—He! You must not force yourself to believe this, but merely face the facts. Listen carefully, be on the alert, and one day you will realize that He is looking at you, speaking to you, challenging you. And then you will enter into unity with Him and act out of this encounter, from this situation of being spoken to and challenged—and that is Providence! You will be not merely thinking but acting. You will be open to God, and Providence will be present.

What does this mean? It means that Providence is not a ready-made machine but is created from the newness of the freedom of God and also from our small human freedom. Not just anywhere, but here. Not just at any time, but now. It is a mystery of the Living God, and you will experience it to the extent that you surrender yourself to it, not letting it merely pass over you, but co-operating with it. You are being called. God is drawing you into the weft of His providential creation. You must realize in your conscience what is at stake. You must set to work with your hands. You must use your freedom. As a living person you must stand within the living activity of God.

The mystery of Providence will not come alive so long as we only think of it intellectually. It will become a reality when we act upon it. Then we shall become aware of the meaning of "The Living God." Then we shall realize this moment of time is new. This situation never existed before. It does not exist in a vacuum of the imagination but within the whole structure of reality. Now you must act as you ought to act. But in freedom. It is God who acts. It is you who act—if I may put it like this with all the due humility of the creature—in agreement with Him. No—take it back. He acts alone. And yet, when God alone is acting, then only are we really ourselves. . . . And that is Providence.

SOURCE: Romano Guardini, *The Living God* (New York: Pantheon Books, 1957), pp. 11–16.

10
Scripture
George Martin

Is the Bible "true and accurate"? Or does it contain many inaccuracies and falsehoods? Before one can answer these questions, one must be conscious of the criteria for determining the "truth" of any piece of writing. Most often, twentieth-century people use the term "truth" as if it were applicable only to items of history. That's not at all correct. "Truth" can be used of poetry, of novels, of fables, if understood properly.

The first criterion for determing the truth of any piece of writing lies in the question: What does the author intend to convey by this particular literary form? The second criterion follows immediately from it and can also be stated in the form of a question: Does what the author intends to convey fit the reality of life?

Let's take the example of a modern novel. The author intends through his story to convey the tragedy of the untimely death of a young wife, married for only a few years. One would miss the point of this piece of writing completely if one tried to figure out if the person of the heroine were based on a real-life celebrity or if one insisted that the setting couldn't have been a city in the east because of the weather conditions mentioned in the novel. The author's intention was not to recount an actual event, not to describe the atmospheric conditions of an eastern city. If the readers understand that the author is trying to expose the universal experience of tragedy in the death of a lover (the first criterion), then they should ask if this novel is true-to-life, if it captures the emotional impact of such an experience, if it lays bare the human reality of suffering and loss and final triumph in such a moment (the second criterion).

George Martin shows us how to apply these criteria to the Bible in the following selection from his book, *Read-*

ing Scripture as the Word of God. Martin has been active in the Catholic charismatic movement and writes a regular monthly column in one of its publications, *The New Covenant* magazine. However, his book does not reflect any of the fundamentalist approach to the Scriptures that is popularly associated with the charismatic movement. He takes into account the up-to-date scholarship and research in the rapidly-progressing field of Scripture studies and puts in a clear, uncomplicated and undefensive way how the Bible came to be written and how we can hear today what God is saying through it.

Even though he is very conscious of the proper methodology involved in an academic and scientific interpretation of the Bible, Martin makes clear that all such scholarship is of little value unless the person can apply the Scripture message to the actual process of living. He thus guides his reader in a pathway between that of the fundamentalist who reads for an immediate, apparent meaning ("It does us little good to eagerly respond to a word from Jesus if we misunderstand it"), and that of the disinterested scholar who studies Scripture as he or she would any other book ("We can have keen insight into the parable of the good Samaritan—but we will not be reading it as the word of God unless we understand how it applies to our own lives").

We Christians believe that we have a written Scripture because God has spoken, and moved human beings to write down the message that he communicated. We believe also that the Holy Spirit continues to speak, as a living voice, through these same written words. It is crucial, therefore, for us to study the Scriptures both in their historical context and in their present application so that we are hearing and responding to God's word and not merely creating a "new word" that we want to hear.

Over the centuries, Christians have taken different views about the complexity of Scripture and the need for study to achieve understanding. One extreme view holds that the Bible is such a difficult and complex book that only professional Scripture scholars can fully understand it. Without knowledge of Hebrew and Greek, an advanced degree in Scripture, and a major commitment of time to study of Scripture, no one can hope to surmount the complexities of Scripture and fully understand it, according to this view.

The error in this approach is obvious. It reduces the word of God to an object for scholarly study, and limits its readers to professional scholars. However valuable professional biblical scholarship is, God's revelation is addressed to more than professional Scripture scholars; it is addressed to every one of us.

On the other extreme is the view that God will speak so simply and directly to the hearts of every reader through Scripture that no problems of understanding will arise. This view holds that since the Bible is the word of God, it must be a word uttered in such a straightforward way that even the simplest person can immediately understand it.

This view has obvious appeal. It recognizes that God's word is addressed to all men, and addressed to them in an understandable manner. However, *it misunderstands how God does speak to man.* Quite often—and quite tragically—adherents of this view fail to hear God properly. In practice, the idea that God speaks simply to the reader of Scripture can mean that Scripture means what it means to me—the individual reader. An "objective" meaning of Scripture becomes elusive. The many sects and denominations who profess to believe "only and all" that Scripture teaches—but who significantly disagree on just what Scripture does teach—should alert us that the matter is not so simple.

The truth lies between these two views.

The Bible does contain God's word to us. But our correct listening to it and understanding of it requires study as well as an open heart. God does not speak to us so simply through Scripture that we can expect to immediately and correctly understand every passage that we read. We must be willing to make an effort to understand the message of Scripture.

Our study of Scripture, and study about Scripture, is both necessary and wise. God does not call all of us to become Scripture scholars, but he does expect us to use the means available to better understand his word to us. Understanding his word requires more than an open heart (although it certainly requires that); understanding his word also requires a willing mind, an eager mind.

Our study of the Bible is an effort on our part to take Scripture seriously. We take it seriously when we are willing to let our lives be remade by what it says; we also take it seriously when we are concerned to find out just what it does say. If we are content to take the first meaning that pops into our head as the "meaning" of Scripture, we not only risk arriving at some very mistaken interpretations, we also show a disregard for Scripture itself. If Scripture has been inspired by God for our reading and instruction, we must respect it enough to be willing to study it.

The Holy Spirit's inspiration is not given to us so that we can forego the normal "human" means to help us understand Scripture. The inspiration of the Holy Spirit is enhanced, not inhibited, by proper study and diligent effort on our part. He does not wish to impart wisdom to us despite our willful ignorance. . . .

However, we should always keep the goal of study in mind. We make the effort to study the Bible (and not merely read it) so we can listen more clearly to the Word of God speaking to us through the words of Scripture. Our study is not for its own sake. We do not study so that we can become experts in the Bible just as some are experts in the history of the American Civil War. Our study is for the sake of our prayerful use of Scripture, so that we may encounter the Word of God there, and find life in that Word.

Our task in reading any book is to understand what its author intended to convey. The first and most important principle of Scripture study is exactly the same: to understand Scripture is to understant what its divine and human authors intended to convey by the words they used, the form they chose, and the ideas they expressed. To understand God speaking through Scripture, we must understand the words of Scripture as they were written under the inspiration of God.

A passage of Scripture means what the author intended it to mean when he wrote it. There can be, to be sure, extended meanings and interpretations given to passages, meanings which go beyond what the author had in mind when he wrote. However helpful and exciting such interpretations may be, they are not the basic meaning of the passage. The basic meaning is that intended by the author. All additional or extended interpretations must be based upon this fundamental meaning and be extensions of it. Extended interpretations are not valid if they are opposed to the basic meaning intended by the author, or if they are held in place of it.

For example, Paul intended to convey something to the Corinthians when he wrote his letters to them. Because Paul wrote under the inspiration of the Holy Spirit, what he intended to convey and what God intended to convey were the same. God did not use Paul to teach something that Paul himself was not aware of when he was writing; God would in effect have been using Paul as an unthinking dictating machine. Rather, the meaning inspired by God was a meaning that Paul himself grasped and intended to write. Paul himself insisted that "There are no hidden meanings in our letters besides what you can read for yourselves and understand."

Reading Scripture in this personal way, as a word speaking to us and about us, does not of course excuse us from the responsibility of study. Unless we have made efforts to understand the meaning of the books and passages of the Bible, we may misunderstand them and misapply them to ourselves. If we fail to grasp the point of a parable, it won't do us any good to try to apply it to our lives.

For example, when Jesus warned the apostles that he was about to be put to death as a criminal and that a time of crisis was at hand, they took his injunction "Let him who has no sword sell his mantle and buy one" (Luke 22:36 RSV) too literally. Their eager reply "Look, Lord, here are two swords" drew a weary rebuke from Jesus; they had misunderstood his words again. It does us little good to eagerly respond to a word from Jesus if we misunderstand it. Therefore, our study of the Scriptures and their meaning is essential.

It is also essential to bear in mind that the meaning of Scripture must become a meaning for us. We can have keen insight into the parable of the good Samaritan—but we will not be reading it as the Word of God unless we understand how it applies to our own lives. "Which of these," Jesus asked, "proved himself a neighbor to the man who fell into the brigands' hands?" We can know the answer to that question quite easily. But the next verse brings the meaning home: "Go, and do the same yourself" (Luke 10:36–37 JB).

SOURCE: George Martin, *Reading Scripture as the Word of God* (Ann Arbor, Michigan: Word of Life Press, 1975), pp. 28–30, 32–33, 60.

11
Sacraments
George S. Worgul

As the following article points out, almost all American Catholics over twenty-five years of age can recite by heart the standard catechism definition of a sacrament, "An outward sign instituted by Christ to give grace." Conversely, almost none of the same group could tell why it is defined that way and where the definition comes from. (That's not a criticism of Catholics over twenty-five, just an objective comment. The origin of the definition has not been taught as part of ordinary Catholic catechesis.)

This definition is derived, not directly from the Scriptures, but from a Greek philosophical analysis of how "causes" work, by a twelfth-century theologian named Peter Lombard. According to Peter, a sacrament is like a chisel in the hands of a sculptor. Although the sculptor is primarily responsible for the finished statue, his work would be impossible without the instrument.

Hence, a sacrament was conceived of as an instrument of grace in the hands of Christ (and in the hands of the human minister). There was some merit to this manner of speaking of a sacrament. It was simple, it explained the causal process with good clarity, it was easy to remember.

However, there is one glaring flaw in such an approach. It can reduce a sacrament to a lifeless instrument! It can give the impression that a sacrament is a "mechanical thing" which, if used properly, produces an automatic result with each usage.

It is this misemphasis that George Worgul attempts to correct in the following article, "What Is a Sacrament?" He points out how a whole set of mechanical images have come to be associated with this definition of sacrament, some of which have been used even in formal written catechesis, e.g., pipelines with grace running through them to fill a container (recipient) at the other end, spiritual gas pumps filling a person up with grace. Such images, we must soberly admit, did lead to a rather "magical" and "slot-machine" conception of a sacrament, at least in the popular mind.

How do we correct this image? Worgul devotes the closing portion of his article to the solution. We must discover a new set of metaphors which clearly demonstrate that a sacrament is primarily a meeting between God and human beings, a coming together of faithful Christians with Christ, their Redeemer. A sacrament is a conscious, active moment, much like the act of love between husband and wife. The metaphor of "instrument" lacks all of the dynamism and personalism that are key to sensing and feeling what happens in the sacramental event.

In the best Christian understanding of sacramentality, all nature is "sacramental," i.e., every physical reality in the universe speaks of a deep internal meaning through its external visible manifestation. Plants and trees speak to us of the incredible process of transforming minerals into living matter; the stars and planets tell us of an almost unbelievable infinitude of complexity beyond us.

The presence on earth of the Son of God as a physical, touchable, space-taking human being *is* the epitome of what a sacrament is. His very being announces the presence of God, reveals what the Father is like. He contains within himself the classic moment of meeting between God and humankind. He is the touchstone of human-divine encounter. Jesus Christ *is* sacrament.

The author of this article, George Worgul, has a first-hand sense of what he writes about. He was continuing education director for the Catholic diocese of Albany for three years, and taught theology at Siena College. Presently he is a member of the theology faculty at Duquesne University.

"A sacrament is an outward sign instituted by Christ to give grace." Most Catholics over 25 will recognize this sentence as the *Baltimore Cathechism*'s definition of A Sacrament. In a rather Pavlovian fashion, the vast majority of Roman Catholics can rattle off the words with supersonic speed. Ask the same vast majority what these words mean and all tapes instantaneously halt. After the initial shock of the question, vague phrases will sputter out blindly searching for an answer. Finally, in desperation, silence will reign supreme. Most Roman Catholics know the words of the definition but their meaning remains elusive.

A first look at the words of the *Baltimore Catechism*'s definition offers hints to its meaning and at the same time raises serious questions. A sacrament is a sign. Sacraments are external, tangible, experiential. They are meant to be perceptible to our senses. These outward signs are said to be instituted by Christ. He is the founder of the sacraments. Sacraments are linked to Him.

Certain questions arise from our first look. Are the sacraments merely signs, purely conventional? Is there any difference between a sacrament and a stop sign? When, where, and how did Christ institute the sacraments? If He instituted seven, why did it take the church until 1215 at the Fourth Lateran Council to reach this conclusion? How do the sacraments give grace? Are they magic? Do they work like a gas pump or a slot machine? Finally, what is grace? Is it something? Is it someone?

The variety and intensity of these questions should make it clear that knowing the words of a definition is only a first step in knowing its meaning. The *Baltimore Catechism*'s definition is fine, but we must judge if a redefinition enables us to more clearly understand what it proposes to explain, a redefinition which at the same time will answer the questions raised above.

The catechism's definition contains four main elements: 1) sign, 2) institution by Christ, 3) give, 4) grace. The redefinition includes each of these four elements. I propose that sacraments are symbols, arising from the ministry of Jesus, which when celebrated in faith are encounters with the living God, Father, Son, and Holy Spirit. The difference proposed in these definitions should not be viewed as purely semantical. The difference lies at the heart of what a sacrament is. There is no verbal whim involved in the choice of new words. The option of new words aims at correcting misconceptions which fester in unknowing minds.

Sign, Image, or Symbol?

A sacrament is a symbol. Symbols are different from both images and signs. An image seeks to exactly reproduce another reality. A photo snapshot or a portrait in oils seeks to capture exactly the face of the person studied. An architect's scale model seeks to exactly depict the structure he will build. The closer an image depicts a reality, the better it is. A sacrament does not reproduce exactly what Jesus did. If we were to strive in this direction, we would celebrate the Eucharist at home during supper; we would not baptize children, since Jesus probably never baptized, etc. Sacraments are not images.

Sacraments are also not signs. A sign points to another reality, but there is no connection between the sign and what it points to. Signs are purely conventional. There is no reason why red means "stop" and green means "go." There is no connection as to why Americans drive on the right side of the road and the English on the left. Society could have just as easily agreed to reverse the order in both instances. Sacraments are more than signs—they are more than mere conventions.

Sacraments are symbols. A symbol is a reality which points to another reality and has the power of making it present, without being identical to it. A symbol lies between an image and a sign. Unlike a sign it is not purely conventional and unlike an image it is not an exact reduplication. Symbols constantly surround us and we use them. Symbols are natural to human existence.

For example, the human body itself is a symbol. The body points to a reality (our total selves) which it is not identical to. Our anger would flare if someone was to treat us as though we were merely or totally our body. We would object that they were ignoring essential parts of our humanity, our psyche, spirit, or personality. We intuitively know that we are more than our bodies. However, our bodies are powerful. They make us present in the world. They enable us to communicate and live. They enflesh our spirit and our consciousness. Our bodies are symbols of our very selves, yet they are not identical to nor do they totally exhaust who we are.

A national flag is a symbol. A flag points to a nation. Flags make the collectivity of a nation present. They summon present the values, history, and goals of a people. The power of this symbol is clearly present when a country has been victorious in the Olympics and its flag is raised high above the others. Yet a flag is not identical to the nation or the country.

A wedding ring is a symbol. The circular band points to and makes present the spouse, the lover, without being identical to the other person. The wedding band symbolizes the bond of love which two people have entered and live within, without being identical to the love relationship which is a reality in their lives.

Food is a symbol. Food points to and makes nourishment and life present without being identical to them. In times of tragedy and natural disaster, countries send food to the afflicted people as a sign of their concern and desire to help. Yet the food is not identical to brotherly love. Food is a symbol of this fellowship.

To say that the sacraments are symbols is to identify them as power-charged realities which possess the energy to make other realities present without being identical to the reality. This is easily seen in Jesus himself who is a symbol. Jesus is the symbol of the Father. He points to and makes the Father present without being identical to the Father. Jesus is the Son of the Father, not the Father himself. The reality which the symbols of the sacraments make present is the living God himself, Father, Son, and Holy Spirit.

Sacraments and Ministry of Jesus

Sacraments are grounded and arise from the ministry of Jesus. There is an essential connection between the sacraments and what Jesus did here among us. Many Catholics erroneously believe that Jesus exactly established each of the seven sacraments. The confusion seems to arise from a narrow understanding of the word "instituted." Instituted can imply that an individual has clearly outlined and defined every phase, step, and form of an action, organization, or program. Institution can also mean that someone lays down the guidelines or principles in an open-ended fashion, leaving the exact form and expression to be set or changed at a later date. The founding fathers of our country instituted our government in the second sense. The founders of many religious orders acted similarly. A historical study shows that Jesus instituted the sacraments in the second sense. In fact, Jesus did not primarily institute sacraments but a community or church. Jesus gathered disciples to himself so that they might continue his ministry by proclaiming the Gospel. Those who heard the Word and believed entered the fellowship.

In reflecting on the ministry of Jesus and the life situation of its members, the church, over a period of time, came to understand that there were special celebrations in the life of the community. These were the sacraments. In the 13th century these sacraments were limited to the seven we now know. Each of these sacraments is bound to an aspect of Jesus' ministry. The Eucharist celebrates the death and resurrection of Jesus, the gift of eternal life to humankind. Baptism celebrates entry into the community founded by Jesus and living according to his Gospel. Confirmation seals in the gift of the Spirit bestowed on those baptized in Jesus' name. Reconciliation celebrates the forgiveness of sins, sins for which Jesus died. Matrimony celebrates the love of Christians bound together in the deepest of human intimacies, a love which models the love of Jesus for his church, his community. Holy Orders celebrates the priestly and prophetic ministry of Jesus, leading his people closer to the Father in prayer and love.

Each of the sacraments is tied to Jesus, the basic and primordial sacrament. All the sacraments and the church itself arise and flow from the one sacrament of the Father, his only Son. The church, in celebrating the seven sacraments, continues Jesus' ministry.

The End of Slot Machine Theology

Since the sacraments arise from the ministry of Jesus and are continuations of that ministry, they are only effective for those who come to believe in Jesus, the Christ. Without this personal decision and commitment of faith, the sacraments are empty and powerless signs. Unfortunately, the faith dimension of sacraments has not been taken seriously by many. When faithlessness exists, sacraments border on, if not enter, the realm of magic. External rites and rituals without internal decision and action produce nothing.

Scholastic theology was well aware of this. Theologians of this school noted two movements in the sacraments: action and faith. These two aspects were expressed as ex opere operato (action performed) and ex opere operantis (faith of the recipient). Neither element can be separated from the other. For many people, the action (going to Mass, pouring water with the proper words, or being anointed by the bishop) was the only important reality. This is clearly a distortion. The faith of the recipient is equally as important and necessary as the action or rite. Without faith there is no sacrament. The canon law of the church forbids the action of the sacrament to be performed if there is reasonable certainty that there is no faith on the part of the recipient of the sacrament. It is precisely faith in Jesus which supplies the meaning of the action being performed.

The word given in the *Baltimore Catechism*'s definition presupposes that those participating in the sacraments actually believe in Jesus. Yet, many Catholics have a very mechanical understanding of the sacraments. One has the impression from many that the sacraments give grace the same way a gas pump gives gas or a slot machine gives coins. For far too many the sacraments are instantaneous and automatic. All the person has to do "to get grace" is be physically present. What is the difference between this attitude and magic? Absolutely none! This magical understanding of sacraments is linked to a misunderstanding of the word "grace," an understanding of grace as something rather than someone.

A Glass Full of Grace

Sacraments give grace. These three words attempt to express one of the deepest mysteries of Christian faith, that God freely and gratuitously offers himself to human persons. A poor choice of models has misdirected the average person's understanding of grace. These models, using physical examples, were reinforced in catechetical books and homilies in the past decades. Today, they remain buried in people's unconscious, going unquestioned, even unknown. An example will make the point clear. In the eighth grade, Sister Immaculata presented the following problem to her class. Jim and Joe are good boys but Jim is the better of the two. They both die and go to heaven. How can they both be perfectly happy, and at the same time Jim be rewarded justly for being better? Sister solved the problem by drawing two figures on the blackboard. One figure, representing Jim, was a large milk glass. The other figure was a little juice glass, representing Joe. Sister then filled both glasses to the brim with chalk. Since both glasses were filled to capacity, both Jim and Joe were perfectly happy. Since Jim's glass contained more "grace," he is properly rewarded and the two parts of the problem are solved.

I cannot object that Sister's presentation does not solve the problem. It does. However, it also creates a problem. The explanation leads us to expect that grace is something. Physical models or examples are only capable of creating physical notions of quantity. I am led to believe that grace is a thing, a thing that I am capable of accumulating more of. Furthermore, a passive attitude toward the sacraments is encouraged by this model. The whole purpose in going to the sacraments is to accumulate more grace. Jim and Joe need do nothing more than be there—if you will, place their glasses in the correct position—and be filled up with grace. The necessity of their personal attention and participation in this explanation is minimal.

The above example does not offer the slightest hint that grace is not something, but someone, this someone being God himself, Father, Son, and Holy Spirit. Yet grace is nothing other than the living, dynamic, personal God. Once grace is understood as God himself, any purely physical model breaks down and fails. Only personal models can help us understand relationships between persons.

Perhaps the best personal model we possess for understanding grace is the love relationship of marriage. The interaction between man and woman employs conversation, touch, silence, active listening, sharing life with one another. Persons who love each other do not merely cohabit in the same place called a house. They are not totally passive. On the contrary, they are active partners—persons pursuing each other, reaching out to each other. The same can be said of friendship. True friends bask in the presence of the other and grow in their love for one another, almost knowing what the other needs or will do before a word is spoken. Where the physical model encourages passivity, the personal model encourages activity and participation.

In the sacraments, the personal God offers himself to us as a friend and lover. The whole mystic tradition of the church agrees to this point, as do the great theologians. God gives himself as a loving Father, a brother in our humanity, a spirit which longs for communion. When we accept God's offer (an action on our part) we accept a personal interrelationship with another living person. Grace in this perspective is not quantitative. It is a deepening, intensifying love with a person. By being people who are grace-filled, that is, filled with the living God, we live a life in greater conformity to the Gospel of the Father's Son through the guidance of his Spirit.

SOURCE: George S. Worgul, "What Is a Sacrament?" *U.S. Catholic,* January 1977, pp. 29–31.

12
Morality
Bernard Häring

Is Christian morality a set of firm rules which, if obeyed faithfully, will lead to a reward in the end—heaven? This has unfortunately been a very common view of Christian moral systems, a view that contains a sufficient kernel of truth to be seriously supported by many Christians and, therefore, vastly misleading. A rules-to-reward notion is not at all the main issue involved in Christian decisions about what is right and what is wrong.

Nor is Christian morality simply a systematic blueprint that teaches one how to perfect oneself. This would make Christian morals the instrument of a very self-centered task (which we discussed in the general introduction to this section).

Neither of these views is adequate for describing the total nature and purpose of Christian moral systems. The reason why Christians distinguish right from wrong is to discover what actions will lead to the heights of human experience, what actions will lead them to taste life fully. According to Bernard Häring in the following selection from his *The Law of Christ,* tasting life fully comes when one is in loving relationship with God.

This loving union with God, which Häring sees as the goal and norm for Christian morality, will of its very nature spill over into every other area of a human being's existence. In the terms of this book, it will give one the foundation for living harmoniously in all of the four basic relationships. Hence, we can say, in this extended sense, that the purpose of Christian morality is to guide people to live a harmonious, peace-filled life, even in the midst of conflict and suffering, understanding that their every action is either a good or a poor relationship with some other facet of reality.

This does not mean that Christian moralists decide on

the goodness or badness of an action "from the standpoint of the profit it brings to man." That is very often unpredictable. No one person can say with absolute certitude that every good action will bring immediately profitable and happy results to the person doing the action. Rather, the Christian moralist concludes that one must trust that, if the action keeps one in loving union with God, it will bear fruit—human and divine—even if we cannot see it or measure it from our human perspective. Christian morality depends ultimately on faith in the value of a loving relationship with God, not on one's ability to measure the apparent success of one's action.

The Law of Christ is Bernard Häring's classic summary of Catholic moral theology. In this work, Häring, a professor of moral theology at the Alfonsianum University in Rome, was one of the first Catholic moralists to attempt to bring the Church's moral teaching back into an integrated whole with its biblical and dogmatic teaching. Since the seventeenth and eighteenth centuries, Catholic moral theology seems to have been a separate science in the Church, with its own autonomous principles. Häring's approach makes the Catholic theologian very conscious once again that moral norms do not come simply from human reasoning, but from listening to the word of God, especially in the Scriptures. He makes us conscious of the fact that the basic question in Christian moral theology is not "What is the best reason I can discover for deciding to do or refrain from doing this action?" but rather "Is this how Jesus taught me to live?"

Although the only rational basis and foundation for true morality is religion, there have been moral efforts and there are moral systems not primarily centered in religion or at least not based on the divine fellowship. What characterizes all these systems? We immediately discard all "scientific" systems of ethics and all pragmatic methods of shaping human conduct which sacrifice the human person to the collective or to any other impersonal end, for they cannot form any serious basis of morality at all. They rather destroy morality. We can take up for serious consideration only the systems which recognize the value of the human person. They all agree in making it the duty of man to perfect himself. For Aristotle, for the Stoic, for Kant and Schleiermacher (to mention only a few), man himself and his own greatness form the foundation of ethics and constitute its goal.

Even though in many instances the existence of a personal God is not formally denied, nevertheless the human person and moral life are not centered in Him. To a degree these systems preserve the earnestness of morality, since they place man in a comprehensive framework of meaning, value, and law to which he must conform. But the ultimate in meaning and goal is always man and his own development and perfection: "The truly noble man never forgets his dignity. He never loses it in things which are inferior to him." The value of all values for him is his own soul, the preservation and development of the worth of his own person. Center of all these ethical systems is man himself. His moral obligation is self-perfection.

If religion exerts influence upon a previously accepted ethical attitude of this kind, the soul is raised to a higher realm of values. Once we have entered into the sphere of the religious, we no longer speak of mere self-perfection, but of salvation of our soul. No matter how extreme the difference between the Indian religious concept of self-purification and the Stoical ethic of self-perfection, the Hindu and all kindred religious orientations are basically nothing more than a projection of the anthropocentric ethic of self-perfection into the sphere of religion.

It is a simple fact that man must think in terms of "person." If God is not thought of as a person or at least if no fellowship is sought with Him, it must inevitably follow that the human person alone can occupy the center of attention. And this is true even when man seeks salvation in the escape from the personal, as in Indian pantheism. Whether the Indian seeks Nirvana as a positive beatitude of a soul which survives after death, or whether he seeks its extinction, the motivation and central meaning of all his asceticism and virtue is man, his own salvation.

Obviously, salvation of soul in the Christian sense is something altogether different. It is not a blessed solitude of existence nor a blissful absorption into an impersonal essence, but loving community with the living God. For this very reason even the Aristotelian or Stoic concept of self-perfection cannot consistently remain projected into an essentially Christian morality. This means that concern for one's salvation may not be centered in self-perfection. The Christian religion as personal fellowship with God cannot tolerate man as center and focal point of ethics.

Viewed in the perspective of religion, the human person can be understood only from the standpoint of personal community and fellowship with God. Nevertheless, as a matter of fact, at least at the beginning of the religious life things are usually different. Particularly the man who at first directed his moral efforts predominantly toward his own perfection is all too readily inclined, once he turns to religion, to seize on it as a means to perfect himself and save his soul. Instead of viewing religion in the proper perspective as first of all a loving community with God and seeking this in fellowship, he sees in it and seeks in it the furtherance and assurance of his own salvation, which flows from such fellowship. If one continues in this attitude, consciously or unconsciously, he closes to himself the surest and deepest approach to God. He disregards the keystone of religion, the holiness of God, which can never be a means to anything, only the end. He loses the sense of loving communion which leads us to eternal bliss only if first and above all else.

Some may object: it is evident that God's glory and loving homage to Him are central in our religious relation to God, but our moral effort is simply directed to man and his salvation! In reply we stress that the effort is indeed concerned with man. This we cannot deny. But must not this very concern for man ultimately be also a concern about God, about obedience to Him, abiding in His love, the coming of His kingdom?

The greatest hazard to genuine religious life arises from making man its center, from viewing all divine worship and all communion with God primarily from the standpoint of the profit it brings to man. But even in the strictly religious activity where such hazard is avoided, there still lurks the danger of a fatal dichotomy between worship and the moral life. Prayer and sacrifice on the one hand have their center and meaning in the divine fellowship, and the moral life is more or less independent—something parallel to or alongside of it—with its ultimate goal man and his salvation. Inevitably the religious and moral life will be estranged and divorced or the man-centered moral orientation will lead to anthropocentric orientation of religion.

The efforts of non-religious man to perfect himself, we must note, are not worthless. They have, in fact, a positive value, at least as long as religion is not dismissed as meaningless. And this positive value can be coordinated with the religious orientation, but not without being reformed, Christianized. In some manner it must be removed from its previous non-religious moorings. To be truly embodied in the realm of the sacred, it must be placed in the service of holiness.

Ultimately morality and religion must have the same center:

community and fellowship with God. This is true both for the scientific presentation of the Christian moral doctrine and for popular instruction and preaching. But unfortunately both the one and the other were too often, especially after the days of the Enlightenment, a continuation of Aristotle (self-perfection) rather than of the Gospel (the sovereignty of God).

We cite only one example chosen from among many: Anthony Koch, a highly esteemed moralist of the Tuebingen school, makes the following significant remark in his moral theology: "Whereas dogmatic theology concerns itself with the nature of God and His external works, with Christ and His Redemptive work, moral teaching has man for its object in as much as it shows him the way prescribed by God to reach his eternal goal." "The aim of moral life is consequently the eternal perfection and the beatitude flowing from it." "According to Catholic moral theology happiness is the goal of all moral endeavor." It is true that this view is poles apart from that of Aristotle, for the simple reason that the Christian cannot attain happiness through his own unaided efforts, but depends for it entirely on God and community of life with God. But precisely because this is presented as something merely accessory or even in a measure extrinsic, or we might say as an afterthought, as though the living friendship with God was only an essential means for the full attainment of the moral purpose—it is evident that the concept of self-perfection or external happiness and salvation cannot be the sound and appropriate foundation for a religious moral system.

Instead of having as its foundation the dialogue between God and man, this system is on the level of the monologue—man to himself and within himself—scheme of morality. Or it is at best, when measured by the standard of the essence of true religion, imperfect dialogue. Dialogue between man and God, word and response, is not basic and essential in this system, but accessory and secondary, something super-added to the monologic morality centering in man.

SOURCE: Bernard Häring, *The Law of Christ* (Westminster, Md.: Newman Press, 1963), Vol. 1, pp. 39–42.

13
Thanksgiving
Michel Quoist

The first reality of biblical history is the gift of God himself and of the gifts from God. Perhaps no motif more adequately reveals the nature of Biblical faith than does thanksgiving for those gifts. The Psalms tell us that to thank God is to be joyful and to proclaim God's wonders and works (Psalm 33:1–3, 21). In 1 Corinthians 1:4–5, St. Paul states:

> I always give thanks to my God for you because of the grace he has given you through Christ Jesus. For in union with Christ you have become rich in all things, including all speech and all knowledge.

Jesus taught—through his life—that the art of thanksgiving is thanksliving or gratitude-in-action: being open, just, caring, courageous.

Not one of us is so destitute that we cannot express our gratitude. Perhaps next to "I love you" the most gracious and appreciated words in the English language are "thank you." For true gratitude, like true love, cannot be commanded or demanded; it must spring spontaneously and freely from the individual.

The word "thank" has an interesting etymology, being derived from an Indo-European base, *tong-,* which came into Latin as *tongere,* "to know." Thus, at the base of gratitude is knowledge. We must be aware of the gifts for which we are appreciative: we must be able "to count our blessings" in order to be thankful.

Most often—and unfortunately—it is the common, ordinary blessings which we fail "to count" or, perhaps, which we take too much for granted. In the next selection, Michel Quoist draws our attention to those common, ordinary blessings. The major portion of the selection is in the form of a prayer. Better yet, it is a meditation on life designed to help Christians discover the rich contact and relationship with God arising from the daily events of our existence.

Michel Quoist is a Catholic priest; he has been a pastor and a chaplain to various young people's Christian Action groups in France; he has a doctorate in social and political science. His book *Prayers*—from which the following selection is taken—has enjoyed phenomenal worldwide success and has been translated into a variety of languages including German, Hungarian, Chinese, Portuguese and Swedish.

Thank You

We must know how to say, "Thank You." Our days are filled with the gifts the Lord showers on us. If we were in the habit of taking stock of them, at night we should be like a "queen for a day," dazzled and happy with so many blessings. We should then be grateful to God, secure because he gives us everything, joyful because we know that every day he will renew his gifts.

Everything is a gift from God, even the smallest things, and it's the sum of these gifts that makes a life beautiful or sad, depending on how we use them.

"All good giving and every perfect gift comes from above, from the Father of the lights of heaven. With him there is no variation, no play of passing shadows." (James 1, 17)

Thank you, Lord, thank you.
Thank you for all the gifts that you have given me today.
Thank you for all I have seen, heard, received.
Thank you for the water that woke me up, the soap that smells good, the toothpaste that refreshes.
Thank you for the clothes that protect me, for their color and their cut.
Thank you for the newspaper so faithfully there, for the comics (my morning smile), for the report of useful meetings, for justice done and for big games won.
Thank you for the street-cleaning truck and the men who run it, for their morning shouts and all the early noises.

Thank you for my work, my tools, my efforts.

Thank you for the metal in my hands, for the whine of the steel biting into it, for the satisfied look of the supervisor and the load of finished pieces.

Thank you for Jim who lent me his file, for Danny who gave me a cigarette, for Charlie who held the door for me.

Thank you for the welcoming street that led me there, for the shop windows, for the cars, for the passers-by, for all the life that flowed swiftly between the windowed walls of the houses.

Thank you for the food that sustained me, for the glass of beer that refreshed me.

Thank you for the car that meekly took me where I wanted to be, for the gas that made it go, for the wind that caressed my face and for the trees that nodded to me on the way.

Thank you for the boy I watched playing on the sidewalk opposite.

Thank you for his roller-skates and for his comical face when he fell.

Thank you for the morning greetings I received, and for all the smiles.

Thank you for the mother who welcomes me at home, for her tactful affection, for her silent presence.

Thank you for the roof that shelters me, for the lamp that lights me, for the radio that plays, for the news, for music and singing.

Thank you for the bunch of flowers, so pretty on my table.

Thank you for the tranquil night.

Thank you for the stars.

Thank you for the silence.

Thank you for the time you have given me.

Thank you for life.

Thank you for grace.

Thank you for being there, Lord.

Thank you for listening to me, for taking me seriously, for gathering my gifts in your hands to offer them to your Father.

Thank you, Lord,
Thank you.

SOURCE: Michel Quoist, *Prayers* (New York: Sheed and Ward, 1963), pp. 61–63.

IV
Relationship with the Material World

Introduction

"World," as used in this chapter, has a double meaning: world is nature, e.g., a tree or stream; and world is nature-transformed-by-humankind, e.g., elements of nature which have been transformed into a building or machine. We humans, of course, have an intimate relationship with the world in this dual sense. In fact, the relationship is so intimate that we are often not aware—let alone appreciative—of the value of this relationship.

It is significant that after Genesis relates the story of human creation, the relationship with the world is immediately and formally bestowed upon humans by God:

> Yahweh God planted a garden in Eden which is in the east, and there he put the man he had fashioned. Yahweh God caused to spring up from the soil every kind of tree, enticing to look at and good to eat. . . . Yahweh God took the man and settled him in the garden of Eden to cultivate and take care of it (Genesis 2:8–9, 15).

We are placed in the garden (relationship with nature), and we are to cultivate and take care of it (which necessitates, to varying degrees, our transforming nature).

In the language of self-understanding, one does not say "I" without referring at least implicitly to one's body as a component of the self. It would seem, also, that one cannot say "I" without referring at least implicitly to one's multifaceted relationship with the material world. I am not the person I am apart from the moon-reflection on the fish-filled river, apart from the bus which takes me to a building where I work. Likewise, I am not the person I am apart from the polluted air I breathe, apart from the recklessly bulldozed and gouged landscape through which I drive.

Further, our relationship with the world is the arena not only for self-understanding but also for maintaining our very existence. For the world (both nature and nature-transformed-by-humankind) provides the sustenance for life and the resources for molding that life.

Nature

Through the ecology movement, people have clearly manifested a concern with caring for the world of nature. Ecology, of course, has taught us about our environment but it has also taught us about ourselves as persons-in-relationships. Ecology makes it quite clear that an understanding of ourselves as separate from the world of nature is not only false but harmful. We humans, like any organism, are inseparable from the processes which surround us and constitute our environment and world.

Theologically, ecology challenges a series of assumptions under which the Judaeo-Christian tradition has long taught us to function; in our relationship with the world our religious tradition (or a misinterpretation of it) has lessened our reverence and respect for nature by emphasizing:

(a) the radical separation between God and nature and between humans and nature;

(b) an eschatology which looks upon the earth as a stepping-stone to a higher plane;

(c) wealth as a sign of divine favor which concept sometimes provided a justification for the abuse of our natural resources.

Nature-Transformed-by-Humankind

We humans are placed in the world of nature and are not only to take care of it but also to cultivate it and to draw out its potentialities. Being in the image and likeness of God (with intellect, imagination, and will, all tempered by love) we are to exercise dominion over the world and to be co-creators of the world with God (Genesis 1:26-29). To exercise dominion and to be co-creators does not mean passivity or "flowing" with nature. A human person, from a Christian point of view, must be actively involved with the world. That involvement, however, is not that of an overbearing taskmaster but of a responsible steward and a covenant partner with the Creator of the world.

Unfolding the potentialities of nature is one of our chief activities as human persons, and it is a primary instrumentality of our own human development. That is, our cultivation or transforming of nature (by growing crops, domesticating animals, using ore to build the Eiffel Tower) not only unlocks the potentialities of nature but also unlocks the potentialities of our very selves.

In order to live with security and dignity in this material environment of physically superior forces, we human beings need to extend and intensify the power of our comparatively feeble body through tools/technology—from flint axes to computers. And clearly, from so doing we have derived notable advantages: shorter work days, faster transporation, marvelous medicines, better housing, instant information, new sources of energy and so on. Yet technology is a mixed blessing: while achieving some worthy ends our use of technology has also precipitated new problems.

In this section, we will consider both the problems and blessings in our relationship with the world, the world of nature and the world of nature-transformed-by-humankind.

14
Theology of Ecology
Edward B. Fiske

In the following selection Edward B. Fiske, as former religion editor of *The New York Times*, expresses his belief that there is, indeed, an ecological crisis. Further, he points the finger of blame for that crisis at our overconcern with individualism:

> The ecological crisis has arisen largely because we have thought primarily in individualistic terms, isolated ourselves from each other as well as from the world around us and compartmentalized our experience.

Part of the solution to the ecological problem is, of course, "cleaner" technology and more laws conducive to sensible, responsible management of our resources. But more importantly, maintains Fiske, there is need for a reevaluation of our religious traditions which might, thereby, free us from that overconcern with self. In other words, a theology of ecology needs to be developed. To the insights of Fiske, we offer the following considerations.

In the Judaeo-Christian tradition, the foundational theory for a theology of ecology—and for a healthy relationship between the human person and nature—is found in the Book of Genesis: God has given the human person dominion or power over nature.

Our dominion over nature is well understood in the context of responsible stewardship. Human persons are to be wise and faithful stewards (Luke 12:42), held accountable for the proper use of the goods of nature. We are not owners but only stewards of the world and its resources. That world has been neither made nor earned by any person or group. It is the Creator's alone: "The earth

94

is the Lord's and the fullness thereof, the world and those who dwell therein" (Ps. 24:1). Poor stewardship is neglecting to care for the material world, assigning to our own particular group exclusive use of one or another of the world's resources, or wantonly destroying these resources. To be concerned only with the present and only with maintaining our own high standard of living is a failure in Christian stewardship. We need to be actively concerned, for example, with the waste of natural resources in order that the goods of nature will be present for future generations.

A theology of ecology must not only be developed; it must also be activated or lived, if only for pragmatic reasons. As we read in Genesis (1:29; 2:15-16), humans are nurtured by nature; without nature providing us with habitat and food, we cannot exist. Nature, however, also nurtures other aspects of our lives by offering us objects and events for aesthetic delight and meditation (see, for example, Psalm 104). Nature offers us companionship (especially of the animals); consolation (a walk in the woods); inspiration for poets and artists. Nature points to God's ongoing self-communication: a here-and-now revelatory presence in time and space. The beginning of Psalm 19 reads, "The heavens declare the glory of God, and the firmament proclaims his handiwork." In a sense, birds and bees, sunsets and moonscapes happen when God expresses himself on our level. The world of nature is one other facet of the Mystery-of-God present. Jesus himself, being true to his Jewish heritage, understood nature as the stage-setting of human redemption and as containing lessons concerning that redemption: the lilies of the field, more beautifully arranged than Solomon in all his glory, were of God's making and were, like the birds of the heavens, fully sustained by God's care. So, too, are his human creatures.

The Christian belief that every element of material creation is a reflection of the creating God—just as every human person is an image of God—leads to a very simple conclusion about our relationship with the world: when the divine instinct in us senses that there is a divine imprint in the tree, the rock, the canyon, we treat that element of nature like "family." We sense a oneness with this material thing because we recognize intuitively that we have the same roots. Respect for and relationship with the world is not a forced experience, nor an attitude that must be superadded to human offspring in the maturing process. It is the exhilarating discovery of the common denominator between humankind and the world of nature.

In the Christian tradition, there have been few persons who have ever achieved the level or relationship with nature attained by St. Francis of Assisi. St. Francis addressed sun and moon, fire and water, plants and animals as his "brothers" and "sisters." He thereby widened the circle of gratitude and love for God and neighbor to include the whole of creation. In our secular age, St. Francis perhaps offers a too romantic approach to nature, but at the very least he stirs the imagination and challenges us to recognize our relationship with, and our dominion over, nature—which can be nothing less than that of responsible stewards. And it is precisely to responsible stewardship that Fiske calls his readers in the following selection.

Several months ago a group of students at San Jose State College, in California, pooled $2,500, bought a shiny new yellow sports car and ceremoniously buried it, to the sound of taps, in a freshly dug grave in the center of the campus. This expensive ritual dramatized the students' belief that the automobile, polluter of the environment, represents a "grave danger to the survival of mankind."

But the students also recognized the car as something more—a symbol of the American Way of Life. As one young woman said: "We're not burying just a piece of metal, but a lot of other things with it."

By their actions the students showed that they know what most of us are beginning to realize in the haziest way: that the current ecological crisis requires not only a few more laws against air pollution but also a fundamental overhaul of our most basic national values and drastic changes in our daily lives. In choosing the traditional burial ceremony to express this the students symbolized too, perhaps unknowingly, the deep connection between ecology and religion and the fact that ecology has become the most crucial religious issue of our day.

Like all cultural and economic systems, ours has been built on a foundation of religious values. Our attitude toward ourselves and our fellow men, our response to the natural world, all are derived from our Judeo-Christian heritage. We believe, for example, in our inherent right to use land, air and water as we choose, to "have dominion over the earth"; in our freedom indeed, our duty to have as many children as we desire, to "multiply and replenish the earth"; in our privilege to acquire as many material belongings as we wish, convinced that the "upright man shall have good things in possession."

Some experts have argued that the beginning of the problem dates from the victory of Judaism, and subsequently Christianity, over paganism. While pagans believed that all objects in nature were endowed with life and thus had profound respect for the natural order, Jews and Christians placed God in the heavens. The result, according to Lynn White, Jr., a historian at the University of California at Los Angeles, was that "Christianity made it possible to exploit nature in a mood of indifference."

While it is true that the Judeo-Christian tradition also contains themes of reverence for the created world, these have not been dominant. Inherent in solving the ecological crisis, therefore, is the development of a fundamentally new religious outlook with new priorities.

The most important element of the new religion must be the recovery of respect for nature. Here we can learn a good deal from the Eastern religions—especially Buddhism, which teaches reverence for all living creatures, and Taoism, which stresses man's harmony and unity with nature. We should concentrate on rediscovering certain of these Eastern attitudes that are latent in our Western heritage. The Creation narrative, the Psalms, the concept of a Sabbath day of rest—all contain positive values of responsibility, stewardship and respect for nature.

Second only to a respect for nature must come a humbler view of man. The Judeo-Christian tradition has emphasized the glory of man, created "in the image and likeness of God" and placed highest in the order of creation. Unfortunately this has carried with it the unquestioned corollary that man is far removed from other forms of life, that plants and animals have value and nobility only insofar as they satisfy human needs. Ecology is now showing us that this view is not only narcissistic, but also potentially suicidal. "To struggle to defend the dignity of man," said theologian Gabriel Fackre, "does not mean one has to denigrate the earth."

A third element of the new religious value system must be a different concept of the relation of man to nature. If man views himself with more humility and views nature with more respect, the two then can coexist as partners, rather than as master and servant. As William McElvaney, a Methodist pastor, put it: "Nature will become man's biospheric colleague, not an environment to be conquered and thoughtlessly exploited." Others have suggested a spaceship metaphor: man and his environment traveling through space on an unknown journey, the functioning of both depending on close cooperation and the constant recycling of limited resources.

Here we might point out that the ecological crisis has emphasized one religious theme that has received little attention in recent time: divine judgment. We do not need a theology of heaven and hell to realize that violation of God's commands to honor His creation carries built-in penalties.

Finally, a religious system capable of meeting the ecological crisis must contain a radically new ethics. For one thing, it has to bring into question our traditional emphasis on individualism. No longer can ethics and law be organized primarily around preserving the rights of individuals. We must recognize crimes against nature and society; we must weigh personal comfort against ecological realities. We must, as we have already noted, challenge the right of every couple to decide how many children to have, in view of the urgent need to control population. We must question an individual's prerogative to utilize limited natural resources, such as seashore property, for private rather than for public use. We must restrict an individual's freedom to possess goods, such as alligator belts and redwood lawn furniture, in order to preserve animal and plant life. In short, we must begin to live by the golden rule, and apply it to our neighbor as well as to the natural world.

The ecological crisis has arisen largely because we have thought primarily in individualistic terms, isolated ourselves from each other as well as from the world around us and compartmentalized our experiences. Institutional religion too has allowed itself to become fragmented over minor doctrinal issues; it has lost sight of common fundamental truths and reduced its ideology to formulas that have little relevance to life as it is actually lived.

But at its best religion is profoundly ecological, for it embraces the totality of an individual's relationships—to himself, to others, to the universe itself—and gives them the unified meaning ecologists say is necessary for the survival of the human race.

Right now, more than any time in recent history, people are searching for religious values that will give meaning to their lives.

Ecology has given our own religious tradition a new and urgent task—to provide the symbols and rituals that will accompany the new values. This should not be a difficult task—traditional religious symbols, like the Garden of Eden, the bread and wine of Holy Communion, can easily be infused with new meaning and made relevant.

Religion and ecology ultimately meet because both stand in judgment against all that is life-denying. Perhaps the mandate they share is that proclaimed by the Lord to Moses in Deuteronomy 30:19: "I call heaven and earth to record this day against you, that I have set before you life and death, blessing and cursing: therefore choose life, that both thou and thy seed may live. . . . "

SOURCE: Edward B. Fiske, "Saving the Earth: A Challenge to Our Religious Traditions," *Redbook*, June 1971, pp.78, 180, 182, 186.

15
Theology of Technology
E. F. Schumacher

A popular theory of ecomomics has insinuated for many decades that "what's good for the economy is ultimately best for the people as a whole." If the gross national product of a country were to increase thirty percent next year, the people of that country would be generally "better off" next year. Expanding economics means a better life for all, materially speaking.

Not so, says E. F. Schumacher, in the following selection from his best seller, *Small Is Beautiful.* He is not simply repeating that old bromide "They may be better off materially but they may be worse spiritually." Not at all! Schumacher maintains that there is no reason to conclude that the people as a whole will be "better off" materially, financially, economically, when the economy of a nation expands. Why? Because our desires-become-needs tend to expand even more rapidly than a healthy economy. More apparently too, the fruits of an expanded gross national product may not touch most of the citizens of a country; it may, indeed, make a significant number of people "worse off" as the rich get richer.

In seeking to give a solution to the problems just raised, Schumacher develops a speculative and practical philosophy of economics. His basic premise is so simple that many readers may immediately say to themselves, "Why didn't I think of that?" His basic premise is that unlimited economic expansion in a limited environment is self-destructive. We live in a limited world. We cannot expect that unlimited development of resources will bring peace, social well-being or any other human benefit, because there can be no such thing as an unlimited development of resources. It is true that we shall always continue to develop new resources but, at any given point in the development, we will be able to measure exactly the limited amount of resources that we possess.

Presently, one consumer in the United States uses fourteen times more energy each day to maintain his or her standard of life than one person in India. In so doing, we consume more than we replace. Can the solution to the subhuman standards of many in India be to "elevate" them to our level of consumption? Hardly. The material resources of this planet would be used up in a flash.

A sound human technology must use the limited materials of the universe in such a way that it replaces what it uses, recreates what it destroys, brings to life other "stuff" to take the place of what it has terminated.

Schumacher's solution to this dilemma, caused by a constant drive for expansion versus limited resources, is at once simple and profound. We must reduce our needs. We must learn to live on less. We can no longer allow, from one age to the next, our luxuries to become necessities.

A Christian theology of technology must begin with the presupposition that, for a technological advance to be genuine, its total effect must be clearly advantageous for the whole living of life. It cannot be merely a more efficient way of doing one procedure that ruins four of five other values in its process (e.g., a scientist develops a substance that makes the packaging of products simpler, and it creates an enormous ecological problem because it cannot be broken down chemically, causes skin cancer in human beings, etc.). Such a process may be momentarily economical, but it is profoundly inhuman, and therefore un-Christian.

Schumacher suggests that an "intermediate technology" may be the bridge between a Christian theory and a reasonable practical growth of the economy. Systems of manufacturing and production that are of a size that a supervisor may be in touch with all parts of the process would not allow us to evade responsibility for the possible bad effects of any portion of the process. Small, indeed, is beautiful.

E. F. Schumacher was a rare combination of economist, practical philosopher, and Christian believer. He

was the economic advisor of the National Coal Board
from 1950 to 1970, and had served as economic advisor
with the British Control Commission after the Second
World War. As director of the Scott Bader Company in
England, he put into practice the principles of economics
enunciated in this selection.

The dominant modern belief is that the soundest foundation of
peace would be universal prosperity. One may look in vain for historical evidence that the rich have regularly been more peaceful than
the poor, but then it can be argued that they have never felt secure
against the poor; that their aggressiveness stemmed from fear; and
that the situation would be quite different if everybody were rich.
Why should a rich man go to war? He has nothing to gain. Are not
the poor, the exploited, the oppressed most likely to do so, as they
have nothing to lose but their chains? The road to peace, it is argued,
is to follow the road to riches.

This dominant modern belief has an almost irresistible attraction as it suggests that the faster you get one desirable thing the more
securely do you attain another It is doubly attractive because it completely bypasses the whole question of ethics: there is no need for re-
nunciation or sacrifice; on the contrary! We have science and
technology to help us along the road to peace and plenty, and all that
is needed is that we should not behave stupidly, irrationally, cutting
into our own flesh. The message to the poor and discontented is that
they must not impatiently upset or kill the goose that will assuredly,
in due course, lay golden eggs also for them. And the message to the
rich is that they must be intelligent enough from time to time to help
the poor, because this is the way by which they will become richer
still.

Gandhi used to talk disparagingly of 'dreaming of systems so
perfect that no one will need to be good'. But is it not precisely this
dream which we can now implement in reality with our marvelous
powers of science and technology? Why ask for virtues, which man
may never acquire, when scientific rationality and technical competence are all that is needed?

Instead of listening to Gandhi, are we not more inclined to listen to one of the most influential economists of our century, the great
Lord Keynes? In 1930, during the world-wide economic depression,
he felt moved to speculate on the 'economic possibilities for our
grandchildren' and concluded that the day might not be all that far

off when everybody would be rich. We shall then, he said, 'once more value ends above means and prefer the good to the useful.'

'But beware!' he continued. 'The time for all this is not yet. For at least another hundred years we must pretend to ourselves and to every one that fair is foul and foul is fair; for foul is useful and fair is not. Avarice and usury and precaution must be our gods for a little longer still. For only they can lead us out of the tunnel of economic necessity into daylight.'

This was written forty years ago and since then, of course, things have speeded up considerably. Maybe we do not even have to wait for another sixty years until universal plenty will be attained. In any case, the Keynesian message is clear enough: Beware! Ethical considerations are not merely irrelevant, they are an actual hindrance, 'for foul is useful and fair is not.' The time for fairness is not yet. The road to heaven is paved with bad intentions.

I shall now consider this proposition. It can be divided into three parts:

First: that universal prosperity is possible;
Second: that its attainment is possible on the basis of the
            materialist philosophy of 'enrich yourselves';
Third: that this is the road to peace.

The question with which to start my investigation is obviously this: Is there enough to go round? Immediately we encounter a serious difficulty: What is 'enough'? Who can tell us? Certainly not the economist who pursues 'economic growth' as the highest of all values, and therefore has no concept of 'enough'. There are poor societies which have too little; but where is the rich society that says: 'Halt! We have enough'? There is none. . . .

Economic growth, which viewed from the point of view of economics, physics, chemistry and technology, has no discernible limit, must necessarily run into decisive bottlenecks when viewed from the point of view of the environmental sciences. An attitude to life which seeks fulfilment in the single-minded pursuit of wealth—in short, materialism—does not fit into this world, because it contains within itself no limiting principle, while the environment in which it is placed is strictly limited. Already, the environment is trying to tell us that certain stresses are becoming excessive. As one problem is being 'solved', ten new problems arise as a result of the first 'solution'. As Professor Barry Commoner emphasises, the new problems are not the consequences of incidental failure but of technological success. . . .

We find, therefore, that the idea of unlimited economic growth, more and more until everybody is saturated with wealth, needs to be seriously questioned on at least two counts: the availability of basic resources and, alternatively or additionally, the capacity of the environment to cope with the degree of interference implied. So much about the physical-material aspect of the matter. Let us now turn to certain non-material aspects.

There can be no doubt that the idea of personal enrichment has a very strong appeal to human nature. Keynes, in the essay from which I have quoted already, advised us that the time was not yet for a 'return to some of the most sure and certain principles of religion and traditional virtue—that avarice is a vice, that the exaction of usury is a misdemeanour, and the love of money is detestable'.

Economic progress, he counselled, is obtainable only if we employ those powerful human drives of selfishness, which religion and traditional wisdom universally call upon us to resist. The modern economy is propelled by a frenzy of greed and indulges in an orgy of envy, and these are not accidental features but the very causes of its expansionist success. The question is whether such causes can be effective for long or whether they carry within themselves the seeds of destruction. If Keynes says that 'foul is useful and fair is not', he propounds a statement of fact which may be true or false; or it may look true in the short run and turn out to be false in the longer run. Which is it?

I should think that there is now enough evidence to demonstrate that the statement is false in a very direct, practical sense. If human vices such as greed and envy are systematically cultivated, the inevitable result is nothing less than a collapse of intelligence. A man driven by greed or envy loses the power of seeing things as they really are, of seeing things in their roundness and wholeness, and his very successes become failures. If whole societies become infected by these vices, they may indeed achieve astonishing things but they become increasingly incapable of solving the most elementary problems of everyday existence. The Gross National Product may rise rapidly: as measured by statisticians but not as experienced by actual people, who find themselves oppressed by increasing frustration, alienation, insecurity, and so forth. After a while, even the Gross National Product refuses to rise any further, not because of scientific or technological failure, but because of creeping paralysis of non-co-operation, as expressed in various types of escapism on the part, not only of the oppressed and exploited, but even of highly privileged groups. . . .

I suggest that the foundations of peace cannot be laid by universal prosperity, in the modern sense, because such prosperity, if attainable at all, is attainable only by cultivating such drives of human nature as greed and envy, which destroy intelligence, happiness, serenity, and thereby the peacefulness of man. It could well be that rich people treasure peace more highly than poor people, but only if they feel utterly secure—and this is a contradiction in terms. Their wealth depends on making inordinately large demands on limited world resources and thus puts them on an unavoidable collision course—not primarily with the poor (who are weak and defenceless) but with other rich people.

In short, we can say today that man is far too clever to be able to survive without wisdom. No one is really working for peace unless he is working primarily for the restoration of wisdom. The assertion that 'foul is useful and fair is not' is the antithesis of wisdom. The hope that the pursuit of goodness and virtue can be postponed until we have attained universal prosperity and that by the single-minded pursuit of wealth, without bothering our heads about spiritual and moral questions, we could establish peace on earth, is an unrealistic, unscientific, and irrational hope. The exclusion of wisdom from economics, science, and technology was something which we could perhaps get away with for a little while, as long as we were relatively unsuccessful; but now that we have become very successful, the problem of spiritual and moral truth moves into the central position.

From an economic point of view, the central concept of wisdom is permanence. We must study the economics of permanence. Nothing makes economic sense unless its continunace for a long time can be projected without running into absurdities. There can be 'growth' towards a limited objective, but there cannot be unlimited, generalised growth. It is more than likely, as Gandhi said, that 'Earth provides enough to satisfy every man's need, but not for every man's greed'. Permanence is incompatible with a predatory atittude which rejoices in the fact that 'what were luxuries for our fathers have become necessities for us'.

The cultivation and expansion of needs is the antithesis of wisdom. It is also the antithesis of freedom and peace. Every increase of needs tends to increase one's dependence on outside forces over which one cannot have control, and therefore increases existential fear. Only by a reduction of needs can one promote a genuine reduction in those tensions which are the ultimate causes of strife and war.

The economics of permanence implies a profound reorientation of science and technology, which have to open their doors to wisdom and, in fact, have to incorporate wisdom into their very structure. Scientific or technological 'solutions' which poison the environment or degrade the social structure and man himself are of no benefit, no matter how brilliantly conceived or how great their superficial attraction. Ever bigger machines, entailing ever bigger concentrations of economic power and exerting ever greater violence against the environment, do not represent progress: they are a denial of wisdom. Wisdom demands a new orientation of science and technology towards the organic, the gentle, the non-violent, the elegant and beautiful. Peace, as has often been said, is indivisible—how then could peace be built on a foundation of reckless science and violent technology? We must look for a revolution in technology to give us inventions and machines which reverse the destructive trends now threatening us all.

What is it that we really require from the scientists and technologists? I should answer: We need methods and equipment which are

—cheap enough so that they are accessible to virtually everyone;

—suitable for small-scale application; and

—compatible with man's need for creativity.

Out of these three characteristics is born non-violence and a relationship of man to nature which guarantees permanence. If only one of these three is neglected, things are bound to go wrong. Let us look at them one by one.

Methods and machines cheap enough to be accessible to virtually everyone—why should we assume that our scientists and technologists are unable to develop them? This was a primary concern of Gandhi: 'I want the dumb millions of our land to be healthy and happy, and I want them to grow spiritually. . . . If we feel the need of machines, we certainly will have them. Every machine that helps every individual has a place,' he said, 'but there should be no place for machines that concentrate power in a few hands and turn the masses into mere machine minders, if indeed they do not make them unemployed.'

Suppose it becomes the acknowledged purpose of inventors and engineers, observed Aldous Huxley, to provide ordinary people with the means of 'doing profitable and intrinsically significant work, of helping men and women to achieve independence from bosses, so that they may become their own employers, or members of a self-governing, co-operative group working for subsistence and a local market. . . . This differently orientated technological progress [would result in] a progressive decentralisation of population, or accessibility of land, of ownership of the means of production, of political and economic power'. Other advantages, said Huxley, would be 'a more humanly satisfying life for more people, a greater measure of genuine self-governing democracy and a blessed freedom from the silly or pernicious adult education provided by the mass producers of consumer goods through the medium of advertisements'. . . .

On the problem of 'scale', Professor Leopold Kohr has written brilliantly and convincingly; its relevance to the economics of permanence is obvious. Small-scale operations, no matter how numerous, are always less likely to be harmful to the natural environment than large-scale ones, simply because their individual force is small in relation to the recuperative forces of nature. There is wisdom in smallness if only on account of the smallness and patchiness of human knowledge, which relies on experiment far more than on understanding. The greatest danger invariably arises from the ruthless application, on a vast scale, of partial knowledge such as we are currently witnessing in the application of nuclear energy, of the new chemistry in agriculture, of transportation technology, and countless other things. . . .

The third requirement is perhaps the most important of all—that methods and equipment should be such as to leave ample room for human creativity. Over the last hundred years no one has spoken more insistently and warningly on this subject than have the Roman pontiffs. What becomes of man if the process of production 'takes away from work any hint of humanity, making of it a merely mechanical activity?' The worker himself is turned into a perversion of a free being.

'And so bodily labour (said Pius XI), which even after original sin was decreed by Providence for the good of man's body and soul, is in many instances changed into an instrument of perversion; for from the factory dead matter goes out improved, whereas men there are corrupted and degraded.'

Again, the subject is so large that I cannot do more than touch upon it. Above anything else there is need for a proper philosophy of work which understands work not as that which it has indeed become, an inhuman chore as soon as possible to be abolished by automation, but as something 'decreed by Providence for the good of man's body and soul'. Next to the family, it is work and the relationships established by work that are the true foundations of society. If the foundations are unsound, how could society be sound? And if society is sick, how could it fail to be a danger to peace? . . .

Economically, our wrong living consists primarily in systematically cultivating greed and envy and thus building up a vast array of totally unwarrantable wants. It is the sin of greed that has delivered us over into the power of the machine. If greed were not the master of modern man—ably assisted by envy—how could it be that the frenzy of economism does not abate as higher 'standards of living' are attained, and that it is precisely the richest societies which pursue their economic advantage with the greatest ruthlessness? How could we explain the almost universal refusal on the part of the rulers of the rich societies—whether organised along private enterprise or collectivist enterprise lines—to work towards the humanisation of work? It is only necessary to assert that something would reduce the 'standard of living', and every debate is instantly closed. That soul-destroying, meaningless, mechanical, monotonous, moronic work is an insult to human nature which must necessarily and inevitably produce either escapism or aggression, and that no amount of 'bread and circuses' can compensate for the damage done—these are facts which are neither denied nor acknowledged but are met with an unbreakable conspiracy of silence—because to deny them would be too obviously absurd and to acknowledge them would condemn the central preoccupation of modern society as a crime against humanity.

The neglect, indeed the rejection, of wisdom has gone so far that most of our intellectuals have not even the faintest idea what the term could mean. As a result, they always tend to try to cure a disease by intensifying its causes. The disease having been caused by allowing cleverness to displace wisdom, no amount of clever research is likely to produce a cure. But what is wisdom? Where can it be found? Here we come to the crux of the matter: it can be read about in numerous publications but it can be found only inside oneself. To be able to find it, one has first to liberate oneself from such greed and envy. The stillness following liberation—even if only momentary—produces the insights of wisdom which are obtainable in no other way. . . .

SOURCE: E. F. Schumacher, *Small Is Beautiful* (London: Abacus Books, 1974), pp. 18–19, 23–30.

V
Relationship with Others

Introduction

Is the perfect moment of human existence the moment of contemplative isolation in which a person stands on a seashore before a magnificent sunset, alone, enraptured, in ecstasy with nature and the God hidden within it? The genuine Christian answer to this rather contrived question is simply—no. There is no ultimate fulfillment in this created condition of ours that does not involve some union with our human brothers and sisters.

There may be ecstatic moments of superlative experience of nature, of God, of pure thinking, when we are alone, but for these experiences to reach their zenith, they must be directed, not just toward self-fulfillment, but in some way to the fulfillment of the human community. (Properly understood, these experiences have their source "from" the human community, e.g., our best thinking comes from the prodding of others.) The solitary mystical experience of God enables one to speak of the Divine more personally, but it also allows us to speak more convincingly to the human community. (St. Benedict tell us that it is the specific *duty* of the contemplative monk "to pass on the fruits of contemplation.") The reverent experience of an untouched scene of nature causes us to treat nature more gently in our complex daily work with thousands of others in the cities—or to invite a loved one to share that same experience so that both our love and the experience are enhanced.

For the Christian, the pinnacle of human experience must include some interrelation, some dialogue, some communion of spirit with other human beings. An idea, a hope, a new movement left inside the mind of its originator, can easily fester and decay, grow stagnant like the backwaters of the woodland stream, if it is not thrust into the sunlight of another person's awareness.

Our human experience readily affirms this. A young woman has experienced deep inside herself a strong conviction about pacifism

109

for years and years, but she has never uttered it to a soul. Quite unexpectedly, at the provocation of two good friends, she spills it out before them. Her conviction is no longer safe and comfortable inside the dark cavern of her own cranium (where it doesn't grow much anyway). As she pours it forth, she sees it in a new way and from a new perspective. It is reflected back to her by other voices, other minds, other hearts. It speeds ahead, it limps, it is buffeted about, it is trimmed. It emerges as thoroughly more mature, though battle-scarred. It has received a new dimension from social intercourse, a communal dimension, an experiential dimension that otherwise would have been lacking.

The ceremony of marriage is an excellent example of this need for social interaction which brings human acts to their fulfillment. The lover feels a great sense of attraction to his loved one and nurtures it within. Gaining in courage, he voices it to her, risking the danger of rejection. His love becomes more real as she responds with like enthusiasm. Gradually his very being calls from within him that he "shout it from the housetops," that he proclaim to the world that this is his "one and only forever." The reality of his love remains weak, unfulfilled, even anemic if he does not enter into this social dimension of reality.

Note how the phrases, "We keep to ourselves," "We mind our own business," "We don't get involved in things like that," have a flavor of narrowness and immaturity about them. The expansion and development that come from plunging into the experiences of others (especially "others" who really are different, in background, nationality, race, social and economic class) will never take place in the lives of those who constantly utter such phrases. Christianity urges involvement, encourages us to take such a plunge. No one dives into the pool of others' experiences without learning to swim a little bit better.

Christianity is a group religion. Jesus revealed it that way. The very instincts of our nature confirm it that way. There is no room in Christinanity for the absolutely isolated hermit whose life never spills over into the lives of his or her brothers and sisters.

16
Self-Giving through Sexuality
Eugene Kennedy

The best gift is the gift of self; so goes an old adage. We give of ourselves when we give the gift of our time. We give of ourselves when we give the gift of our heart—love and forgiveness; of our mind—ideas and dreams; of our words—encouragement and inspiration; of our body—vitality and beauty.

One mode of offering this total gift of self is through sexual-sharing. A common misconception is that sexual-sharing entails simply the gift of body. On the contrary, it involves the total person—body, intellect, emotions, imagination. Further, a most rewarding and fascinating aspect of human sexual-sharing is that in giving of oneself, one receives the gift of the other person. In sexual-sharing there is, of necessity, relationship. Sexuality is the Creator's ingenious way of calling people constantly out of themselves and into relationship with another.

In this light, it is inadequate to say that the function of sex is simply for the propagation of the species, or merely for the purposes of tension-release or physical pleasure. Sexual-sharing liberates a person from a mere self-oriented striving and leads the person to encounter with another, where both might grow in self-realization and in the arts of giving selflessly and receiving graciously.

Traditionally, the most favorable context for this giving and receiving of self has been marriage. The expressions used in the Genesis account of Eve's creation—"it is not good that man should be alone," "helpmate," "bone of my bones and flesh of my flesh," "two in one flesh"—summarize a biblical vision of marriage. Indeed, for the Christian, it is marriage itself which has served to symbolize the loving bond of commitment that joins God and his people (Ephesians 5:32).

It would seem, then, that sexual-sharing is enriched in

meaning and comes close to its full human significance from the commitment, respect, support, and equality of marriage partners. It is the marriage context which provides the time for love to unfold and deepen; conjugal sexual-sharing seems to best give expression to mutual affection, enabling the partners to be more sensitive to each other, more concerned, more selfless, more tender, more cheerful and generous—all affecting the readiness to bring new life into the world and aiding the upbringing of those already born.

Eugene C. Kennedy—author of the following excerpt—is a psychologist and professor of psychology at Loyola University of Chicago; he is also the author of over twenty-five books, dealing mainly with counseling. In this excerpt, Kennedy places sexual-sharing forcefully in the arena of relationships which are open, trusting, and an expression of self-giving—the best gift.

. . . In his sexual behavior, attitudes and fantasies, man says a lot about himself. Probably the most significant thing man's management of his sexuality indicates is the degree of his overall growth and development. It is true for man in general and for man in particular: sexuality is expressive and reflective of how fully human he is.

Man has really only recently begun to listen carefully to the message of his sexuality. He has, of course, always been fascinated by it, as the phallic shards of ancient monuments and the remnants of his first love poems tell us. But man has had to live through centuries made dark by ignorance and emotional inhibition. He did not cease to be sexual during these times. The indirect, hypocritical or symbolic forms of sex that abounded during Victorian-like eras revealed the sharp edges and the deep shadows of the classic puritan profile. So too the much heralded sexual liberation of our day tells us something about the maturity of man on the verge of a new century. Man's sexuality and the complex of feelings he has about it reflect his attitudes toward himself and toward his neighbor. His sexual behavior tells us whether his reaching out to others is tender and respectful or clutching and selfish; it reveals whether man is growing or not in true friendship and love.

Sexuality fits into the human framework of love, completing it and setting it off from all other human experiences. Healthy sexuality doesn't come out of diet foods, fun-in-the-sun-nudity or exciting new patent medicines. It flourishes when two people love one another and keep working at developing their relationship with one another despite the pile-up of life's problems. Sexuality is full of sunrise when lovers have been able to work their way through the darkness of misunderstandings and new learning that are so much a part of their lives. Sexuality that arises from a growing relationship keeps on growing itself. That is why it is such a revealing sign of man as he is found in the human condition, man always in process, man trying to move forward in growth. . . .

The common denominator for the present symbolic sexual expression of man is found in man's estrangement from friendship and love. When he is confused about the meaning of these, it shows up clearly in his sexuality. The dropping of repressive defenses just makes it easier for us to see this. For example, the present passion for the quick uninvolved and uninvolving sexual episode documents the inability of most people to take on the responsibility of relationship with another. A recent French survey revealed that men were showing a new preference for the isolated and emotionally uninvolving experience of sex-variety rather than richness being the key element. The tradition of the mistress is being eroded by this trend, precisely because it demands some kind of consistency and continuity in responsible relationship. Much better, then, the experience without antecedent or consequent emotional claims. The quick "score," our language catching the cold mathematics of it, can be preferred only by men who do not want to be bothered by the challenge of love. They clearly separate sex from relationship in this kind of experience, isolating themselves as the friendless generation that searches for but does not find fulfillment. This kind of person points, by his sexual behavior, to the real problem of undeveloped human relationships that lies beneath it.

The person who thus isolates sex from the meaning it can have only when his total self is engaged with others never deals with the challenges that are the vitalizing aspects of love. He need not learn the meaning of faithfulness, for example, because there is no one to whom he commits himself. He need not hope because, just as episodic sex has no past, neither has it any future. He does not love because he has insulated himself from the flow of life with others, which is its only setting. Man hung-up on self-saving and self-defeating sex as isolated pleasure stifles the impulse to relate to others because love dangerously demands that he continue to grow. All the potential meaning of human relationships, the whole direction in which man must go if he is to fulfill himself, is brought into focus by his restlessness and lack of deep satisfaction with this kind of behavior. . . .

An overlapping area of our culture finds a new celebration of the human body on stage, screen, and in newer forms of the encounter group styles of therapy. Outlandish and immature as this often is, it is at least a move away from regarding the body as a prison for the spirit. It is also a sign of man's efforts, barely conscious to himself, of trying to re-establish the unity of human personality. Man is, in other words, blundering toward a mature value through a whole range of immature behaviors. The point is that the steps to maturity are necessarily immature. The problem arises, as it does in the present, when man settles for or gets stuck at some midpoint on the ladder of development, and when no one really helps him with understanding or assistance to complete his journey. Sadly enough, much of the nudity in entertainment reflects the somewhat fragile and two-sided effort man makes to be at home in his own body. Much of it is developmentally narcissistic and homosexual, a celebration, in Walter Kerr's phrase, of impotence rather than of the mature power appropriate to sharing and giving life. It is an effort to feel whole again, an attempt to rediscover the profound significance of touching, and being touched, of that subtle communication that necessarily involves man's body. The full realization of the meaning of the psychosomatic unity of the person is attained only in the far reaches of authentic friendship and love. There man and his body are more comfortably one, and his integrated sexuality is truly expressive of his unity.

When man suffers in some way that he will not face or cannot put directly into words, he plays a dumb-show of his inner pain to himself and to the world. This expresses his problem symbolically. Those who would help man must decode these symbols and strive to assist him to overcome the obstacles and conflicts that hinder his growth. The Church has not only lost touch with man who struggles this way; it has contributed to the isolation of sexuality from love and the meaning of human relationships. It has been, as a human institution grown creaky, insensitive to man's symbolic sexuality. This is a betrayal of its own healthy Gospel traditions, which are lighted up by a great wisdom and appreciation of human sexuality. The Church's involvement in this problem is coming to light because it is being challenged to come closer to man, to enter more deeply into his life, to be friend rather than a master to him. In this challenge to relate more closely to man the Church's failure to integrate its sexuality has become more obvious. Indeed, in no area has it spoken more confusedly in recent years than it has in terms of man's sexuality. It has revealed an outdated vocabulary as well as a divided and suspicious model of man. The institutional Church's failure to keep up with man has shown up in sexuality.

The difficulty is that the Church is only beginning to shake loose from the paralysis of the centuries. In fact, the struggles of the Church to come alive again show up in sex too. The discussions of birth-control and celibacy are first cousins to the other sexual symbolism of our time. They are signs of men trying to understand their sexuality and of attempting to reintegrate it into a fully developed picture of themselves. The discussions indicate man's search for the dimensions of life that give support and meaning to human sexuality. These dimensions are, of course, friendship and love, the only elements that enable man to put himself fully together. They are, needless to say, deep Gospel values as well, but values that, for one reason or another, became like a foreign language on the tongues of many churchmen.

I think that the Church is attempting to recover its lost view of man but that it will have increased difficulty in doing this until it can admit just how much it has contributed to the separation of sex from love. The Church did further this separation, however, with great thoroughness and with tremendous force. Sex, as has been commented on often enough, was seen not as a healthy part of growing man but as something marred, something less than good, something tolerated for preserving the race. So, too, the Church kept people at a distance from one another, making them uneasy about their own bodies and their sexual powers, and in the process, accentuating their estrangement from what was fully human. Somewhere along the line, the very idea of the deep and healthy meaning of bodily contact was sicklied with the pale cast of suspicion. The wonder that lovers should know of the confirming and nourishing power of their bodily communication was checked by a generation of churchmen who elevated *noli me tangere* to the level of a counsel if not a commandment. Other examples, already mentioned by numerous observers, such as the overevaluation of virginity and the great suspicion of friendship and intimacy, are significant because they contributed so powerfully to the isolation of sex from the human experience of love. Without giving further examples, it is enough to note the widespread and controlling effect of this non-integrated view of the human person. It was multiplied, after all, in pronouncements from pulpits, the application of canon law, and the pervasive effects of a widespread educational system. Now the Church is not the chief or only villain, to be sure. But, as the instrumentality charged to preserve a thorough understanding of man, it grew distracted or sleepy and failed to sense just what a distorted and unhealthy image of man and his sexuality it absorbed in the course of time. The Church came not to be the champion of spontaneous and loving relationships but the guardian of careful and controlled ones; it became not the preserver and integrator of man's basic relationships to himself and his neighbor, but an agency that divided and estranged man from friendship and love. . . .

The Church has, in any case, contributed a good deal, and quite unconsciously, to the problem. It remains for it to come fully to terms with it so that it can help all men rediscover the meaning of friendship and love.

This is the task of all the Churches, the proclamation of the Gospel that unites man in the love that is the life of God. And a chief task for any Church is the creation of the environment of community that has its roots in the Gospel vision of man whose destiny is to achieve the highest level of human development in the integrating experience of love. Man's yearning for this is expressed in his struggling efforts to integrate all the aspects of himself, including his sexuality.

The message has many levels and a mixture of meanings: man yearning for the light that evaporates fear and for the freedom to be himself; man confused and cowed by the pain of relationships unreached or gone sour; man tangled in the shredded but enticing web of primitive sexual experiences; man hung-up on reaching other persons in a trusting and loving way. Human sexual behavior, like litmus paper in a chemical reaction, sensitively reflects man in process, man trying to muster up his real identity from a tragically disordered set of experiences.

What shows up in sex in our era does not express a new maturity as much as it does man's shuffling and sometimes sideways movements in his struggle to grow. Man is, in some overall sense, growing in a gangling and uncoordinated way, somewhat the way all adolescents do. His intelligence is extraordinary and his muscles ripple across the earth he has tamed. Emotional growth has not, however, kept pace, and so man suffers adolescent problems. He looks grownup, but he is unsure of himself inside; he is fascinated by the throbbing strength of his sexual powers, but he is also afraid and uneasy about them; he wants to touch others in the mysterious relationships of friendship and love, but he is shy and awkward; he is made to be a man, but in an instant, he can revert to less-developed forms of relationships, destroying tenderness with aggression, alienating himself from what he wants and needs most: open and trusting relationships. . . .

Authentic sexual freedom comes about only in the lives of those who can see sexuality as a vital aspect of their relationship with other persons. These people do not look at sex as the end of all loneliness or the automatic open sesame of human relationship. They know that friendship and love precede and irradiate sexuality as a deeply appropriate and expressive aspect of man. But this knowledge does not come easy, or all at once; it gets deeper only as it unfolds across the years. Friendship and love are a fabric made strong by the strands of suffering and patience, understanding and sensitivity, living and dying that are in its weave. People who have begun to learn the lessons of friendship and love can at last see sexuality in its place, which is considerably less than the whole horizon of life. Indeed, until we take trust and human sharing more seriously, our ears will be filled with the language of sexual liberation, but our hearts will feel painfully empty of the love that really makes us free.

SOURCE: Eugene Kennedy, "Sex and the Modern Christian," in *Sex: Thoughts for Contemporary Christians,* ed. Michael J. Taylor (Garden City, N.Y.: Doubleday, 1972), pp. 63–64, 66–74.

17
Work
Wolfhart Pannenberg

Why does the ordinary person go to work each day?
The probable answer that most people would give to this
question is to earn money to support oneself and one's
family. If this is the accurate answer it could easily mean
that the ordinary working person is not conscious of value in the work itself, but only of value in the monetary
return that work brings.

Is this indeed true? Has our modern highly-industrial-
ized, technological work system created such a mental-
ity? Perhaps it has, according to Wolfhart Pannenberg in
the following excerpt from his book, *What Is Man?* Perhaps our modern system has so dehumanized work that
most of us feel that we "cannot afford" to pursue a work-
life that we find personally interesting and fulfilling.

Pannenberg does not suggest that we scrap the whole
system and go back to a social order wherein each person
is a craftsman, a creative individual who personally fashions an entire "craft-object" which he or she personally
enjoys or sees others immediately use and enjoy. Such
"ancientism" is neither possible nor desirable in a society
that has over eight million people living in a single city
like New York or Tokyo.

He suggests rather that, in the division of labor (e.g., in
a mass-production factory, in a complicated sales system), each of us be taught to see our role as "service to
the whole." Each of us must understand that we are co-
creators in the process of transforming God's world. Can
the person who inserts a single bolt into a new Dodge
Dart take pride in the finished product? Can a salesperson feel a sense of accomplishment in selling a temperature-control system to a company whose operation will
be made more efficient and ecologically sound thereby?
Pannenberg concludes that they not only can but must

feel this way if their work is to be genuinely human, genuinely divine.

More important, is it possible that the assembly-line worker could consider the sound construction of the auto to be equally as important as his or her paycheck? Could the salesperson consider the effectiveness of the temperature-control system to be equally as valuable as a large commission? These are tense questions. The following article implies that, unless we as workers can do this, work is dehumanized, is divorced from its most meaningful dimension, is rendered a lifeless mechanical procedure—like a slot machine that spews out a barrage of coins as the result of a successful spinning of gears.

In order that work remain genuinely human each worker in a complex work-process must be able to affirm the whole of the common task as his or her own. One Japanese auto assembly plant invites all the workers to come to the end of the assembly to touch and inspect the finished product each day. An English textile firm invites its employees to do the same thing.

Pannenberg makes one other interesting observation that deserves special notice. Presently in our modern socio-economic system, more people are defined by their use of leisure than by the choice of work-position. If the amount of compensation is the primary determinant of the jobs people choose, then the real self can come out only when the compensation is not present. What are you? Examine your leisure, Pannenberg says, to discover this.

Wolfhart Pannenberg is a professor of systematic theology at the University of Munich in Germany. *What Is Man?* is one of his earlier and more popular works. It was originally a series of lectures broadcast over the North German Radio Network. He has also written several scholarly works which have gained for him a reputation as a leading creative thinker in modern theology. His most well-known scholarly work in English translation is *Jesus: God and Man.*

There is a connection between the relationships men have with one another and their involvement with the world of things. There may be scarcely any configuration of human community that is not connected with material interests. However, there also is scarcely any mastery of the material world that is not, at least under the surface, socially conditioned. Mastery of the world of nature and of the cultural world, which must be transformed repeatedly, interacts with social relationships as a historical process, which always produces new stages in the shaping of human life. In this process man's relation to nature is interwoven more and more into the social relationships between men. I call this the social process. Through it men are united with one another and with nature by their cooperative subjection of nature.

We now want to consider what significance the social process has for man's destiny. As we saw earlier, man's destiny is directed toward attaining the wholeness of his own existence. This wholeness is not possible apart from the unity of his world and apart from community with other men. Thus, the social process appears to be the path along which man's destiny is to be sought.

But whether the social process really brings man closer to his destiny or estranges him from it is a much-discussed question. It is not only in Rousseau's call for a return to nature that culture and civilization appear to be erroneous paths. But then there are the thinkers who regard the history of society as humanity's progress toward the creation of their true nature. Marx tied both ideas together. On the one hand, Marx thought that the present social relationships would not allow men to arrive at true humanness. On the other hand, however, he expected the realization of genuine humanness through a revolution in these relationships.

For us Marx's expectation seems to be a utopia. However, the problem of Marxism is not yet settled, even if we understand that it does not lie in man's hands to actualize his humanness, and even if we are persuaded that a person can receive what is essential only from God. The question still remains as to whether social relationships do not signify a dehumanization, that is, an alienation of man from his destiny. If the social relationships render man's humanness impossible, then a revolution in these relationships would be required as a humane deed. Then all other humanity would be a mere illusion. Therefore, since Marx, an alive awareness of man is no longer possible without entering into the question of the human significance of the social process.

Marx saw the fall into sin as occurring in the division of labor among different individuals which had taken place in the remote primeval era of social history. The consequence of the division of labor was the division of possessions and, further, the emergence of relationships of domination and oppression of man by man. . . .

In order to understand this judgment it is necessary to consider the human significance of work somewhat more exactly. Work is not something that is independent of man's human existence. Like all activity, it is always a manifestation of a man's nature. Like all behavior, work brings something to expression. Our moods and our character can be read out of our attitudes and movements. Where our behavior changes something in our surroundings, leaving traces, these traces reveal something about our selves. All activity that produces something is thus a manifestation of a man's essence. What that means in human terms is possibly shown most clearly in recreational production. The person at recreation experiences himself in the work produced. . . .

Men change the things in their natural surroundings by arranging them for the satisfaction of their needs. The knowledge that man is able to obtain about himself from the world also changes in the process. Man changes the things around him, and in doing so he simultaneously changes the standard by which he judges his own nature. Therefore, it is not a matter of indifference that no one but himself causes the changes in the things around him. From the things that have been transformed, man perceives himself differently than before, and he also perceives himself as the one who was able to produce such changes. Through his products he learns what he is capable of doing; in this sense the young Marx could say, "Activity is . . . self-creation . . . ."

Man perceives himself not only in terms of the thing he produces, but also in terms of what he comes across and what he is dependent upon. Man always perceives himself as dependent on something before which he stands: beyond the world on God and within the world itself on the material basis for all technological development. He is dependent on the social and intellectual traditions out of which he lives, even where he turns against them. He is dependent on what happens to him from day to day and from hour to hour without his cooperation. He is dependent on the men who are with him, and upon everything that is given to him through them. In all that and beyond that he is dependent on God.

Marx also can speak elsewhere in a profound way about the individual's dependence on other men. This dependence on other men, however, throws a light on the social division of roles, and the consequences of this division, that allows for the emergence of an aspect entirely different from what Marx described. Each person is dependent on other men, and only together with others can he strive for the one destiny of man. Therefore, each person also shows a lively interest in the creations of other people. For that reason, the need of other men's products is not necessarily alienation. Rather, the possibility for exchange with others offers the individual an enrichment of his own nature. This is certainly the case in intellectual as well as in material matters.

To be sure, the incoporation of the individual in the tasks of the community makes him one-sided in his particular role. However, as long as he affirms this community and is gladly a member of it, he also participates in the achievements of the other members of the community, and he experiences their attainments proudly as his own success.

Thus, the division of labor and exchange by no means always signifies alienation and loss of man's essence. That happens only when the individual is no longer able to look beyond his own particular role, when he can no longer affirm his role as a service to the whole, and when he limits himself to his one-sided function, which then must in fact become meaningless. It is here that the real problem lies. The question is whether the whole of a community is still in view in all the division of labor, and whether the total task in which the individual cooperates can still be affirmed as a concern of all the participants, not just as the interest of an individual who enslaves the others. Only to the extent that each cooperating person is able to affirm the common task as his own work does he know himself with his own particular task to be participating meaningfully in the whole which he serves, but which also sustains him. . . .

SOURCE: Wolfhart Pannenberg, *What Is Man?* (Philadelphia: Fortress Press, 1970), pp. 110–113, 117–118.

18
The Family
Henri J. M. Nouwen

Henri J. M. Nouwen, the author of our following selection, was born and educated in Holland, where he was ordained a Catholic priest in 1957. He has taught at the University of Notre Dame, Yale Divinity School, and several institutions in Latin America and Holland.

In his book *Reaching Out*—from which this excerpt is taken—Nouwen maintains that the best possible and most satisfying life entails a continual "reaching out"—a stretching toward our innermost self, toward God, and toward our fellow human beings.

Nouwen states that "reaching out" to our fellow human beings involves "hospitality," which "means primarily the creation of a free space where the stranger can enter and become a friend. . . . [Hospitality] wants to create . . . a friendly emptiness where strangers can enter and discover themselves as created free" (p. 51).

This understanding of hospitably reaching out to others is, of course, fundamental to healthy relationships in the family—the crucial unit within society and the attention of much Christian writing today. The biblical experience of the family was so important and meaningful that its use was extended to apply to Israel viewed as a covenant community under God. Early Christian writers continued the use of this figure by speaking of Christians as comprising "God's family" (1 Tim. 3:15; 1 Pet. 4:14).

The family is important because within it various generations come together and are meant to help one another grow in wisdom and love. As family members interact, they learn to harmonize rights and responsibilities. The family is thus the primary agency in which persons learn to care for each other.

Of course, the role of parents in the family is central. For, in a very real sense, parents "create" persons by loving them into being, from conception onward. But precisely because familial relationships are so close, they are sometimes taken for granted. Parents, for example, sometimes fail to provide their children with those simple courtesies and gracious considerations which they might readily extend to the stranger. Sometimes the parents' desire for the child's "best" limits the child's healthy searching and experimentation. Or, even more insidious, a parent's need to live through the child stifles that child's own life and potential.

In the following selection, Nouwen addresses himself to the family relationship of parent-to-child and offers some perceptive suggestions for the enhancement of that relationship.

It may sound strange to speak of the relationship between parents and children in terms of hospitality. But it belongs to the center of the Christian message that children are not properties to own and rule over, but gifts to cherish and care for. Our children are our most important guests, who enter into our home, ask for careful attention, stay for a while and then leave to follow their own way. Children are strangers whom we have to get to know. They have their own style, their own rhythm and their own capacities for good and evil. They cannot be explained by looking at their parents. It is, therefore, not surprising to hear parents say about their children, "They are all different, none is like the other and they keep surprising and amazing us." Fathers and mothers, more than their family and friends, are often aware how their children differ from themselves and each other. Children carry a promise with them, a hidden treasure that has to be led into the open through education (e=out; ducere=to lead) in a hospitable home. It takes much time and patience to make the little stranger feel at home, and it is realistic to say that parents have to learn to love their children. Sometimes a father or mother will be honest and free enough to say that he or she looked at the new baby as at a stranger without feeling any special affection, not because the child was unwanted but because love is not an automatic reaction. It comes forth out of a relationship which has to grow and deepen. We can even say that the love between parents and children develops and matures to the degree that they can reach out to each other and discover each other as fellow human beings, who have much to share and whose differences in age, talents and behavior are much less important than their common humanity.

What parents can offer is a home, a place that is receptive but also has the safe boundaries within which their children can develop and discover what is helpful and what is harmful. There their children can ask questions without fear and can experiment with life without taking the risk of rejection. There they can be encouraged to listen to their own inner selves and to develop the freedom that gives them the courage to leave the home and travel on. The hospitable home indeed is the place where father, mother and children can reveal their talents to each other, become present to each other as members of the same human family and support each other in their common struggles to live and make live.

The awareness that children are guests can be a liberating awareness because many parents suffer from deep guilt feelings toward their children, thinking that they are responsible for everything their sons or daughters do. When they see their child living in ways they disapprove of, the parents may castigate themselves with the questions: "What did we do wrong? What should we have done to prevent this behavior?" and they may wonder where they failed. But children are not properties we can control as a puppeteer controls his puppets, or train as a lion tamer trains his lions. They are guests we have to respond to, not possessions we are responsible for.

Many parents question the value of baptism of newborn babies. But one important aspect of early baptism is that when the parents bring their child to the church, they are reminded that the child is not their own private property but a gift of God given to a community that is much larger than the immediate family. In our culture it seems that all the responsibility for the child rests on the biological parents. The high-rise apartment buildings, in which families live in their small isolated units and are often fearful of their neighbors, do indeed not offer the small child much more to depend on than his own parents.

During a visit in Mexico, sitting on a bench in one of the village plazas, I saw how much larger the family of the children was. They were hugged, kissed and carried around by aunts, uncles, friends and neighbors, and it seemed that the whole community spending its evening playfully in the plaza became father and mother for the little ones. Their affection, and their fearless movements made me aware that for them everyone was family.

The church is perhaps one of the few places left where we can meet people who are different than we are but with whom we can form a larger family. Taking our children out of the house and bringing them to the church for baptism is at least an important reminder of the larger community in which they are born and which can offer them a free space to grow to maturity without fear.

The difficult task of parenthood is to help children grow to the freedom that permits them to stand on their own feet, physically, mentally and spiritually and to allow them to move away in their own direction. The temptation is, and always remains, to cling to our children, to use them for our own unfulfilled needs and to hold on to them, suggesting in many direct and indirect ways that they owe us so much. It indeed is hard to see our children leave after many years of much love and much work to bring them to maturity, but when we keep reminding ourselves that they are just guests who have their own destination, which we do not know or dictate, we might be more able to let them go in peace and with our blessing. A good host is not only able to receive his guests with honor and offer them all the care they need but also to let them go when their time to leave has come.

SOURCE: Henri J. M. Nouwen, *Reaching Out* (Garden City, N. Y.: Doubleday and Co., Inc., 1975), pp. 56–58.

19
The Church and Liturgy
Cyprian Vagaggini

As is obvious from the other articles in this section, Christianity is not an individualistic religion. It does not allow one to remain isolated from the rest of the human community. Christianity is a group religion. Jesus called his followers to be a "holy people," not simply "holy individuals."

This is as true for Christians at prayer and worship as it is in social action. To pray as a community is not optional. It does not depend on individual taste or preference. To assemble as a worshiping congregation is part of the specific revelation of Jesus of Nazareth. This is the principal reason why it is so important to have one day set aside each week for calling the Christian community together for prayer and praise of God.

Communal prayer and worship are not universally important in the religions of the world. Many pagan cults from Greco-Roman times found it satisfactory to have a priest standing alone at a shrine, offering a sacrifice to a god in behalf of the community. A classical Buddhist could find the peak experience of religion alone in meditation. But not even a Trappist monk in Christianity can claim to have no need for the community celebration that has evolved from the Last Supper.

Note the term that we purposely used in the last sentence—"celebration." What images does that bring to your mind? Crowds of smiling people, enjoying one another's company? A beautifully decorated table overflowing with a cornucopia of fresh, delectable foodstuffs? An event being recalled and presently enjoyed in the same spirit by all who are present? If these are some of the images that fill your consciousness, then you are thinking accurately about Christian liturgy. Becuase of our American usage, the terms "ritual" and "ceremony" have a lifeless ring to them. "Celebration" evokes the sense of vivacity, hope and wonder that belong to Christian worship. To believe that God is present among us, to have an appreciation of the goodness of his creation, to be grateful for the supportive friendships of those close to us, cannot be a routine event. No wonder we call liturgy "celebration."

Dom Cyprian Vagaggini, one in a long line of great Benedictine liturgical scholars at the College of San Anselmo in Rome, calls liturgical worship a "law" in Christianity. In the following selection from *Theological Dimensions of the Liturgy,* he insists that it is inherent in the Divine Will that human beings praise God in a group, that they pray together in community. Human beings simply cannot attain their fullest human spiritual development unless they are part of a worshiping community.

Since liturgy, in the Catholic tradition, includes the seven sacraments, Vagaggini gives a careful analysis of how each sacrament expresses a special relationship to the Christian community, and thereby makes a unique contribution to the development of the individual Christian.

Revelation acquaints us with a most important aspect of the aims and plans designed by God in His dealings with men. The aspect of which we speak is this: in communicating His divine life to the world, He has not just willed to draw to Himself a certain number of individuals, each considered separately from the others as so many atoms; rather, it has been His design to found a city, a divine organic society, a people of God, a kingdom of God. Thus, single individuals cannot attain to the supernatural level nor can they reach the mode of existence which God has willed for them; they cannot have a supernatural existence at all, nor can they even develop themselves, except in close connection with and dependence, even physical, upon this community, this people, as God has effectively planned it. This is the law of salvation in community.

An immediate consequence of this law is that, in the supernatural area, conflict between the good of society and the good of the individual is simply impossible, because these two goods formally coincide and, by God's free will, they constitute but a single solitary supernatural good of the individual and of society—or better, of the individual in society. . . .

By the general law of salvation in community is understood the

ultimate dimension of the fact that only such a sacramental and hierarchical priesthood, acting in virtue of its mission, has the power, in
the liturgical action, to transform an assembly of men into something
immeasurably more profound than an aggregate of many individuals,
believers though they be, into the sacral actualization (sacrificial,
sacramental, prayerful) of the mystical body of Christ; into that people of God willed by God Himself and listened to by Him, in His
whole plan for men; into an *ekklesia* which in the liturgical action is
reunited as such to Christ, who is really present in person or in power, under the veil of the sensible signs of His ministers in the liturgical rites. In the liturgical action the single individual participants are
actualized or become always more actualized as members of this reality, of the higher and divine order, which is the body of the Church
united to its Head and vital principle, Christ.

This is why we say, as we explained in a previous chapter, that
in the liturgical reality it is always the Church as such who acts,
while her individual members act only insofar as they are her ministers and members, or members only; that is, insofar as they are included in the ecclesial reality, as Church, as family, as people of
God. And that is why the divine efficacy of the liturgical action immeasurably surpasses the proper power personally inherent in the individuals who perform that action or who are in attendance
thereat. . . .

Theologically speaking, every liturgical action is always of a
profoundly communitarian nature. . . .

. . . The Mass by its very nature and by its ritual structure is essentially an action of the whole ecclesial community, and most especially of that part which is present *hic et nunc.* What is treated of is,
of course, the action of a community differentiated and hierarchically organized into its individual members and its individual ranks,
each having its own specific part to play, without a confusion and
without an equalization of roles. Nevertheless, it is always a unified
action of a single community whose members are all active in working out a single drama which concerns all and in which all have an
active role, each in his own way. In ancient times, therefore, there
was no conception at all of some members or of some ranks of the
community being present at the Mass only as spectators or simply as
listeners. Still less was it conceivable that they should be occupied in
meditation or private prayer with no connection or at best with but a
loose connection with the action that was being dramatized as the action of all. . . .

Something similar to what has just been said in regard to the

Mass in respect to the ritual expression of its communitarian nature might also be said in regard to the sacraments. The intrinsic communitarian nature in each of the individual sacraments is no less evident than it is in the Mass. The sacraments, in fact, are something ecclesial, because they are the instruments of the grace by means of which, supernaturally speaking, the faithful are born, are nourished, are protected and perfected by the Church and in the Church, as organic members of the people of God, hierarchically structured and differentiated.

Thus baptism is not only the supernatural regeneration of an individual (Rom. 6:1–14) and his adoption as a son of God, but at the same time it is also and necessarily his visible initiation into the body of Christ which is the Church, thereby effecting his supernatural organic union with the other differentiated members of the same body. Nor does baptism constitute union with Christ, except in the Church and by means of the Church, hierarchically structured and differentiated.

Confirmation is not only the supernatural perfecting of an individual; it is also a perfecting of his being included in the people of God.

Penance is not only the reconciliation of an individual with God, but at the same time it is also and necessarily his reconciliation with the Church, with the community of the brethren whom the sinner offended and injured at the same time that he offended God.

That holy orders and matrimony have a deeply communitarian character is obvious and well-known, since they are destined immediately to provide for the material and spiritual multiplication of Christian society and for the formation of its hierarchical structure.

It would not be difficult for the historian to show how in the administration of these sacraments the ancient ritual expression brought their communitarian nature under strong emphasis, and how, contrariwise, in the practice of recent centuries, in consequence of various historical developments, this communitarian expression was frequently somewhat diminished or even obscured; as a result, in some cases the communitarian aspect has become clouded over in the psychology of the faithful.

For baptism and confirmation we have but to recall the ancient ritual of Christian initiation, performed solemnly only once or twice in the year, during the vigils of Easter and Pentecost, in the presence of the ecclesial community of the place presided over by the bishop who, as head of the *ekklesia,* introduced new members into the sacred community of the brethren. In such an atmosphere there was a very lively sense of the significance of the act of Christian initiation as an act of Holy Mother Church, who gives birth to new members; of the body of Christ, which aggregates to itself new cells; of the annual conscription of Christ's holy army.

If, on the other hand, we think of the usual manner in which baptism is administered, it will be obvious that there had been a diminution, in our psychological outlook, of its value as act of initiation and of entrance into an ecclesial community, an act which is of interest to the community as a whole. Today in a baptism, even in the best Christian families, everything seems to be limited to the concept of the regeneration of a soul or, if you will, to a family festival. The communitarian ecclesial aspect which the ceremony carries with it is barely perceived.

Penance is the sacrament which for us has the most studiously private character. The whole is limited to a matter between ourselves and God, in which the priest, it is true, acts as intermediary and as minister, but in which we perceive only with difficulty anything of a communitarian ecclesial character. In the administration of the sacrament of penance, everything is private and secret: private confession, private absolution, private penance.

Contrariwise, in antiquity and up to the period of the sixth to the eighth centuries, when a change in discipline in regard to penance was effected, we find no sure evidence—the opinions of some to the contrary notwithstanding—of private sacramental penance for other than private sins, while there is ample evidence of public penance for public sins. This discipline of public penance involved confession, which, at least implicitly, was public for grave and notorious sins, which were submitted for deliberation to the ecclesiastical assembly presided over by the bishop with his presbyters and deacons and in the presence of the people; the excommunication of the sinner who "has sinned so grievously that he is cut off from communication in prayer and assembly and from every holy transaction"; public works of penitence or satisfaction, among which was the custom of prostrating oneself with tears not only before the bishop and the presbyters, but even before all the brethren of the community; the public reconciliation accorded by the bishop in the presence of the whole community of the brethren, as a re-admission to peace not only with God, but also and necessarily with the Church and with the brethren.

Basic to this discipline, of course, is the concept that sin is not only an offense against God but also and at the same time an offense damaging to the whole *ekklesia,* which, therefore, is a thing of concern to the whole community. . . .

It is also known that in ancient times, at least in some places, the communitarian character of the sacrament of holy orders was rendered even more evident than it is today, through the effective intervention of the whole concerned community in the designation of candidates for the episcopate, priesthood, and diaconate of a specific church. Something of this is still in evidence today in the posting of the banns before diaconate and priesthood, and in the investigations that precede episcopal election.

In the rite of the sacrament of matrimony the expression of its communitarian nature has been maintained substantially intact; and in a certain respect it has even been strengthened—by the prescribing of an obligatory form and by the declaring of clandestine marriages invalid. Nevertheless, in certain regions and in certain classes of society, there is a strong tendency to avoid as much as possible the celebration of matrimony in the parish church and to search out chapels and smaller remote country churches, where every effort is made to obtain the intimate atmosphere of a restricted audience, rather than before the whole *plebs Dei* as represented by the ecclesial cell which the parish constitutes. . . .

SOURCE: Cyprian Vagaggini, *Theological Dimensions of the Liturgy* (Collegeville: Liturgical Press, 1976), pp. 277, 282, 284, 285–286, 293–295, 297.

20
The State
Walter M. Abbott, ed.

In the medieval world, the ideal relationship of the Christian person to the state was quite simple. It was a relationship of basic obedience and trust, as long as the state was faithful to Christian teaching as expressed by the Church of the times. In the Holy Roman Empire, Church and state were so intimately related that faithfulness to one was most often faithfulness to the other.

This was not only a fact but also an ideal. Many medieval theologians concluded that the fullness of human life on earth would be achieved in a political community in which any distinction between Church law had withered away. This came to be known as the "organic" theory of government. The government, the Church, the family together espouse one set of ideals and work for the full development of each individual.

There is one great limitation to an organic theory of government. Of its very nature, it can allow for only *one set of ideals.* Different people striving for different ideals would disrupt the smooth organic concept of one unified whole.

The organic theory of the political community is not espoused in the following selection. The bishops of the Catholic Church, at the Second Vatican Council (1962–65), had moved far beyond that medieval theory when they wrote the document, "The Church in the Modern World," from which this excerpt has been taken. They propose, rather, the "mechanistic" concept of a state which allows for many sets of ideals and many different political philosophies to exist in the same community. The mechanistic theory proposes that it is *not* the purpose of the state to develop the ideal human individual. The purpose of the state is to provide the circumstances in which persons may ideally develop themselves!

In this view, the state does not have one ultimate set of ideals for human fulfillment. It has instead a concept of ideal conditions, ideal circumstances, in which "individuals, families and groups can achieve their own fulfillment." For example, in the United States of America, one could not say that the ideal citizen is a Democrat, of European extraction, Protestant, a liberal capitalist, and middle class. There can be no such classifications. The ideal citizen can only be, very generally, a person who is wisely pursuing his or her own ideals while promoting the common good and respecting the rights of all others.

Lest one conclude that only a constitutional democracy can be a bedfellow with this mechanistic notion of the state, the selection points out carefully that any form of government which respects the freedom of individuals can be consonant with the mechanistic view. It is certainly true that there is a great affinity between the principles of a democratic state and the Christian notion of the "freedom of the children of God," but this freedom may be—and is—found in other political forms. It is errant theology to conclude that the teachings of Jesus lead politically only to a democracy.

It is encouraging to note that the fathers of Vatican II were willing to be quite optimistic about the art of politics itself. In a pessimistic post-Watergate American political scene, it is heartening to hear the almost two and a half thousand Catholic bishops of the world urge young people to take part in "the difficult but honorable art of politics."

This selection is from the Second Vatican Council document, "The Church in the Modern World" (Latin title, *Gaudium et Spes*). It was carefully and painstakingly composed in the fourth session of the Council in 1964, and has become the most famous of the Vatican II documents no doubt because it addresses many concrete problems that continue to weary us today.

From a keener awareness of human dignity there arises in many parts of the world a desire to establish a political-juridical order in which personal rights can gain better protection. These include the rights of free assembly, of common action, of expressing personal opinions, and of professing a religion both privately and publicly.

For the protection of personal rights is a necessary condition for the active participation of citizens, whether as individuals or collectively, in the life and government of the state.

Among numerous people, cultural, economic, and social progress has been accompanied by the desire to assume a larger role in organizing the life of the political community. In many consciences there is a growing intent that the rights of national minorities be honored while at the same time these minorities honor their duties toward the political community. In addition men are learning more every day to respect the opinions and religious beliefs of others. At the same time a broader spirit of cooperation is taking hold. Thus all citizens, and not just a privileged few, are actually able to enjoy personal rights.

No better way exists for attaining a truly human political life than by fostering an inner sense of justice, benevolence, and service for the common good, and by strengthening basic beliefs about the true nature of the political community, and about the proper exercise and limits of public authority.

Nature and Goal of Politics

Individuals, families, and various groups which compose the civic community are aware of their own insufficiency in the matter of establishing a fully human condition of life. They see the need for that wider community in which each would daily contribute his energies toward the ever better attainment of the common good. It is for this reason that they set up the political community in its manifold expressions.

Hence the political community exists for that common good in which the community finds its full justification and meaning, and from which it derives its pristine and proper right. Now, the common good embraces the sum of those conditions of social life by which individuals, families, and groups can achieve their own fulfillment in a relatively thorough and ready way.

Many different people go to make up the political community, and these can lawfully incline toward diverse ways of doing things. Now, if the political community is not to be torn to pieces as each man follows his own viewpoint, authority is needed. This authority must dispose the energies of the whole citizenry toward the common good, not mechanically or despotically, but primarily as a moral force which depends on freedom and the conscientious discharge of the burdens of any office which has been undertaken.

It is therefore obvious that the political community and public authority are based on human nature and hence belong to an order of things divinely foreordained. At the same time the choice of government and the method of selecting leaders is left to the free will of citizens.

It also follows that political authority, whether in the community as such or in institutions representing the state, must always be exercised within the limits of morality and on behalf of the dynamically conceived common good, according to a juridical order enjoying legal status. When such is the case citizens are conscience-bound to obey. This fact clearly reveals the responsibility, dignity, and importance of those who govern.

Where public authority oversteps its competence and oppresses the people, these people should nevertheless obey to the extent that the objective common good demands. Still it is lawful for them to defend their own rights and those of their fellow citizens against any abuse of this authority, provided that in so doing they observe the limits imposed by natural law and the gospel.

The practical ways in which the political community structures itself and regulates public authority can vary according to the particular character of a people and its historical development. But these methods should always serve to mold men who are civilized, peace-loving, and well disposed toward all—to the advantage of the whole human family.

Political Participation

It is in full accord with human nature that juridical-political structure should, with ever better success and without any discrimination, afford all their citizens the chance to participate freely and actively in establishing the constitutional bases of a political community, governing the state, determining the scope and purpose of various institutions, and choosing leaders. Hence let all citizens be mindful of their simultaneous right and duty to vote freely in the interest of advancing the common good. The Church regards as worthy of praise and consideration the work of those who, as a service to others, dedicate themselves to the welfare of the state and undertake the burdens of this task.

If conscientious cooperation between citizens is to achieve its happy effect in the normal course of public affairs, a positive system of law is required. In it should be established a division of governmental roles and institutions and, at the same time, an effective and independent system for the protection of rights. Let the rights of all persons, families, and associations, along with the exercise of those rights, be recognized, honored, and fostered. The same holds for those duties which bind all citizens. Among the latter should be remembered that of furnishing the commonwealth with the material and spiritual services required for the common good.

Authorities must beware of hindering family, social, or cultural groups, as well as intermediate bodies and institutions. They must not deprive them of their own lawful and effective activity, but should rather strive to promote them willingly and in an orderly fashion. For their part, citizens both as individuals and in association should be on guard against granting government too much authority and inappropriately seeking from it excessive conveniences and advantages, with a consequent weakening of the sense of responsiblity on the part of individuals, families, and social groups.

Because of the increased complexity of modern circumstances, government is more often required to intervene in social and economic affairs, by way of bringing about conditions more likely to help citizens and groups freely attain to complete human fulfillment with greater effect. The proper relationship between socialization on the one hand and personal independence and development on the other can be variously interpreted according to the locales in question and the degree of progress achieved by a given people.

When the exercise of rights is temporarily curtailed on behalf of the common good, it should be restored as quickly as possible after the emergency passes. In any case it harms humanity when government takes on totalitarian or dictatorial forms injurious to the rights of persons or social groups.

Citizens should develop a generous and loyal devotion to their country, but without any narrowing of mind. In other words, they must always look simultaneously to the welfare of the whole human family, which is tied together by the manifold bonds linking races, peoples, and nations.

Let all Christians appreciate their special and personal vocation in the political community. This vocation requires that they give conspicuous example of devotion to the sense of duty and of service to the advancement of the common good. Thus they can also show in practice how authority is to be harmonized with freedom, personal initiative with consideration for the bonds uniting the whole social body, and necessary unity with beneficial diversity.

Christians should recognize that various legitimate though conflicting views can be held concerning the regulation of temporal affairs. They should respect their fellow citizens when they promote such views honorably even by group action. Political parties should foster whatever they judge necessary for the common good. But they should never prefer their own advantage over this same common good.

Civic and political education is today supremely necessary for the people, especially young people. Such education should be painstakingly provided, so that all citizens can make their contribution to the political community. Let those who are suited for it, or can become so, prepare themselves for the difficult but most honorable art of politics. Let them work to exercise this art without thought of personal convenience and without benefit of bribery. Prudently and honorably let them fight against injustice and oppression, the arbitrary rule of one man or one party, and lack of tolerance. Let them devote themselves to the welfare of all sincerely and fairly, indeed with charity and political courage.

Politics and the Church

It is highly important, especially in pluralistic societies, that a proper view exist of the relation between the political community and the Church. Thus the faithful will be able to make a clear distinction between what a Christian conscience leads them to do in their own name as citizens, whether as individuals or in association, and what they do in the name of the Church and in union with her shepherds.

The role and competence of the Church being what it is, she must in no way be confused with the political community, nor bound to any political system. For she is at once a sign and a safeguard of the transcendence of the human person.

In their proper spheres, the political community and the Church are mutually independent and self-governing. Yet, by a different title, each serves the personal and social vocation of the same human beings. This service can be more effectively rendered for the good of all, if each works better for wholesome mutual cooperation, depending on the circumstances of time and place. For man is not restricted to the temporal sphere. While living in history he fully maintains his eternal vocation.

The Church, founded on the Redeemer's love, contributes to the wider application of justice and charity within and between nations. By preaching the truth of the gospel and shedding light on all areas of human activity through her teaching and the example of the faithful, she shows respect for the political freedom and responsibility of citizens and fosters these values.

The apostles, their successors, and those who assist these successors have been sent to announce to men Christ, the Savior of the world. Hence in the exercise of their apostolate they must depend on the power of God, who very often reveals the might of the gospel through the weakness of its witnesses. For those who dedicate themselves to the ministry of God's Word should use means and helps proper to the gospel. In many respects these differ from the supports of the earthly city.

There are, indeed, close links between earthly affairs, and those aspects of man's condition which transcend this world. The Church herself employs the things of time to the degree that her own proper mission demands. Still she does not lodge her hope in privileges conferred by civil authority. Indeed, she stands ready to renounce the exercise of certain legitimately acquired rights if it becomes clear that their use raises doubt about the sincerity of her witness or that new conditions of life demand some other arrangement.

But it is always and everywhere legitimate for her to preach the faith with true freedom, to teach her social doctrine, and to discharge her duty among men without hindrance. She also has the right to pass moral judgments, even on matters touching the political order, whenever basic personal rights or the salvation of souls makes such judgments necessary. In so doing, she may use only those helps which accord with the gospel and with the general welfare as it changes according to time and circumstance.

Holding faithfully to the gospel and exercising her mission in the world, the Church consolidates peace among men, to God's glory. For it is her task to uncover, cherish, and ennoble all that is true, good, and beautiful in the human community.

SOURCE: "The Church Today" (Chapter IV: The Life of the Political Community), Walter M. Abbott, ed., *The Documents of Vatican II* (New York: America Press, 1966), pp. 283–298.

21
The World Family
Julius K. Nyerere

In our relationship with others, we find ourselves as members not only of a family, a church, a nation but also of the world family which transcends race, religion, and national boundaries. Indeed the Fatherhood of God implies the brotherhood and sisterhood of all peoples. And each one of us has responsibilities in that world family: primarily to insure that all people can satisfy their basic needs so that they may truly *live* their lives.

This is the context for the following selection, which is an address to the 1970 General Assembly of the Maryknoll Sisters. The address was written and delivered by the President of Tanzania, Julius Nyerere. A son of a chief from one of Tanzania's tribes, Nyerere converted to Catholicism at the age of twenty-two; he has been referred to as the "conscience of Africa."

Nyerere notes that our present world family is tragically divided along economic lines: the very rich and the very poor. He challenges Christians to face that reality, to abandon any overemphasis on "life in the world to come," and to see the present world as an arena of struggle. The struggle is to bring about social change which will enable all human persons to be truly "the image and likeness of God." President Nyerere states:

> I am suggesting that, unless we participate actively in the rebellion against those social structures and economic organizations which condemn men to poverty, humiliation, and degradation, then the Church will become irrelevant to man and the Christian religion will degenerate into a set of superstitions.

Nyerere reflects several strands of contemporary Christian theologizing which might be termed "liberation theology," a movement developed in Latin America and spreading among Christians particularly in third world countries. There are two major components of liberation theology: (1) the scriptural concerns with justice as found in the Old Testament prophets and with empathy and service as delineated, for example, in Matthew 25; and (2) the Marxist analysis of why there is oppression in the world.

Liberation theology seeks to articulate and make operative or real the liberation/freedom themes found in the exodus and resurrection motifs of Scripture. Liberation theology implies liberation *from* all forms of oppression (sin)—economic, social, political, cultural, psychological. It implies liberation for enabling human persons to be the "new man" described in St. Paul's Letter to the Colossians.

Against this background we can see with greater clarity the relevance of Christ as liberator. Christ comes to liberate human persons from sin. Sin is spelled out concretely in terms of alienation, dehumanizing poverty, illiteracy, malnutrition and all that keeps us from reaching full human potential and interaction as understood, for example, in the four basic relationships.

Poverty is not the real problem of the modern world. For we have the knowledge and resources which could enable us to overcome poverty. The real problem—the thing which creates misery, wars and hatred among men—is the division of mankind into rich and poor.

We can see this division at two levels. Within nation states there are a few individuals who have great wealth and whose wealth gives them great power; but the vast majority of people suffer from varying degrees of poverty and deprivation. Even in a country like the United States, this division can be seen. In countries like India, Portugal or Brazil, the contrast between the wealth of a few privileged individuals and the dire poverty of the masses is a crying scandal. And looking at the world as a collection of nation states, we see the same pattern repeated. There are a few wealthy nations which dominate the whole world economically, and therefore politically; and a mass of smaller and poor nations whose destiny, it appears, is to be dominated.

The significance about this division between the rich and the poor is not simply that one man has more food than he can eat, more clothes than he can wear and more houses than he can live in, while others are hungry, unclad and homeless. The significant thing about the division between rich and poor nations is not simply that one has the resources to provide comfort for all its citizens, and the other cannot provide basic services. The reality and depth of the problem arises because the man who is rich has power over the lives of those who are poor, and the rich nation has power over the policies of those which are not rich. Even more important is that our social and economic system, nationally and internationally, supports these divisions and constantly increases them, so that the rich get ever richer and more powerful, while the poor get relatively ever poorer and less able to control their own future.

This continues despite all the talk of human equality, the fight against poverty, and of development. Still the rich individuals within nations, and the rich nations within the world, go on getting richer very much faster than the poor overcome their poverty. Sometimes this happens through the deliberate decision of the rich, who use their wealth and their power to that end. But often—perhaps more often—it happens "naturally" as a result of the normal workings of the social and economic systems men have constructed for themselves. Just as water from the driest regions of the earth ultimately flows into the oceans where water is already plentiful, so wealth flows from the poorest nations and the poorest individuals into the hands of those nations and those individuals who are already wealthy. A man who can afford to buy only one loaf of bread a day contributes to the profit accruing to the owner of the bakery, despite the fact that the owner already has more money than he knows how to use. And the poor nation which sells its primary commodities on the world market in order to buy machines for development finds that the prices it obtains, and the prices it has to pay, are both determined by the "forces of the free market" in which it is a pigmy competing with giants.

> For he that hath, to him shall be given; and he that hath not, that also which he hath shall be taken away from him.

Both nationally and internationally this division of mankind into the tiny minority of rich, and the great majority of poor, is rapidly becoming intolerable to the majority—as it should be. The poor nations and the poor peoples of the world are already in rebellion against it; if they do not succeed in securing change which leads towards greater justice, then that rebellion will become an explosion. Injustice and peace are in the long run incompatible; stability in a changing world must mean ordered change towards justice, not mechanical respect for the status quo. It is in this context that development has been called another name for peace.

Man Is the Purpose

The purpose of development is man. It is the creation of conditions, both material and spiritual, which enable man the individual, and man the species, to become his best. That is easy for Christians to understand because Christianity demands that every man should aspire towards union with God through Christ. But although the Church—as a consequence of its concentration upon man—avoids the error of identifying development with new factories, increased output, or greater national income statistics, experience shows that it all too often makes the opposite error. For the representatives of the Church, and the Church's organizations, frequently act as if man's development is a personal and "internal" matter, which can be divorced from the society and the economy in which he lives and earns his daily bread. They preach resignation; very often they appear to accept as immutable the social, economic, and political framework of the present-day world. They seek to ameliorate intolerable conditions through acts of love and of kindness where the beneficiary of this love and kindness remains an object. But when the victims of poverty and oppression begin to behave like men and try to change those conditions, the representatives of the Church stand aside.

My purpose is to suggest to you that the Church should accept the fact that the development of peoples means rebellion. At a given and decisive point in history men decide to act against those conditions which restrict their freedom as men. I am suggesting that, unless we participate actively in the rebellion against those social structures and economic organizations which condemn men to poverty, humiliation and degradation, then the Church will become irrelevant to man and the Christian religion will degenerate into a set of superstitions accepted by the fearful. Unless the Church, its members and its organizations express God's love for man by involvement and leadership in constructive protest against the present conditions of man, then it will become identified with injustice and persecution.

If this happens, it will die—and, humanly speaking, deserve to die—because it will then serve no purpose comprehensible to modern man.

For man lives in society. He becomes meaningful to himself and his fellows only as a member of that society. Therefore, to talk of the development of man, and to work for the development of man, must mean the development also of that kind of society which serves man, which enhances his well-being, and preserves his dignity. Thus, the development of peoples involves economic development, social development, and political development. And at this time in man's history, it must imply a divine discontent and a determination for change. For the present condition of men must be unacceptable to all who think of an individual person as a unique creation of a living God. We say man was created in the image of God. I refuse to imagine a God who is poor, ignorant, superstitious, fearful, oppressed, wretched—which is the lot of the majority of those He created in His own image. Men are creators of themselves and their conditions, but under present conditions we are creatures, not of God, but of our fellow men. Surely there can be no dispute among Christians about that. For mankind has never been so united or so disunited; has never had such power for good nor suffered under such evident injustices. Men's capacity has never been so clear, nor so obviously and deliberately denied.

The world is one in technological terms. Men have looked down on the earth from the moon and seen its unity. In jet planes I can travel from Tanzania to New York in a matter of hours. Radio waves enable us to talk to each other—either in love or abuse—without more than a few seconds elapsing between our speech and the hearing of it. Goods are made which include materials and skills from all over the world—and are then put up for sale thousands of miles from their place of manufacture. Yet at the same time as the interdependence of man is increased through the advance of technology, the divisions between men also expand at an ever-increasing rate. The national income per head in the United States is said to be more than $3,200 a year; in Tanzania it is approximately $80—i.e. it would take a Tanzanian 40 years to earn what an American earns in one year, and we are not the poorest nation on earth. Further, it has been estimated that, while the rich countries are adding approximately $60 a year to the per capita income of their citizens, the average increase of per capita income in the poor countries is less than 2 dollars per year. It has been estimated that up to 500 million people on the earth today are suffering from hunger—from never having enough to eat. Further, one out of every two of the world's peoples is suffering from malnutrition—from deficiencies of protein or other essential health-giving foods. And finally, let me remind you that even within the wealthiest countries of the world, the misery and oppression of poverty is experienced by thousands, or even millions, of individuals, families, and groups.

So the world is not one. Its peoples are more divided now, and also more conscious of their divisions, than they have ever been. They are divided between those who are satiated and those who are hungry. They are divided between those with power and those without power. They are divided between those who dominate and those who are dominated, between those who exploit and those who are exploited. And it is the minority which is well fed, and the minority which has secured control over the world's wealth and over their fellow men. Further, in general that minority is distinguished by the color of their skins and by their race. And the nations in which most of that minority of the world's people live have a further distinguishing characteristic—their adoption of the Christian religion. These things cannot continue, and Christians, above all others, must refuse to accept them. For the development of men, and the development of peoples, demands that the world shall become one and that social justice shall replace the present oppressions and inequalities.

Man Is a Member of Society

In order to achieve this, there must be economic development and equitable distribution of wealth. The poor nations, the poor areas, and the poor peoples must be enabled to increase their output; through fair distribution they must be enabled to expand their consumption of the goods which are necessary for decency and for freedom.

For what is required is not simply an increase in the national income figures of the poor countries, nor a listing of huge increases in the production of this crop or that industry. New factories, roads, farms, and so on, are essential; but they are not enough in themselves. The economic growth must be of such a kind, and so organized, that it benefits the nations and the peoples who are now suffering from poverty. This means that social and political development must go alongside economic development—or even precede it. For unless society is so organized that the people control their own economies and their own economic activity, economic growth will result in increased inequality, both nationally and internationally. Those who control a man's livelihood control a man; his freedom is illusory and his equal humanity is denied when he depends upon others for the right to work and to eat. Equally, a nation is not independent if its economic resources are controlled by another nation; political independence is meaningless if a nation does not control the means by which its citizens can earn their living.

In other words, the development of peoples follows from economic development only if this latter is achieved on the basis of the equality and human dignity of all those involved. And human dignity cannot be given to a man by the kindness of others. Indeed, it can be destroyed by kindness which emanates from an action of charity. For human dignity involves equality and freedom, and relations of mutual respect among men. Further it depends on responsibility, and on a conscious participation in the life of the society in which a man moves and works. The whole structure of national societies and of international society is therefore relevant to the development of peoples. And there are few societies which can now be said to serve this purpose; for there are few—if any—which both accept, and are organized to serve, social justice in what has been called the Revolution of Rising Expectations.

Let us be quite clear about this. If the Church is interested in man as an individual, it must express this by its interest in the society of which those individuals are members. For men are shaped by the circumstances in which they live. If they are treated like animals, they will act like animals. If they are denied dignity, they will act without dignity. If they are treated solely as a dispensable means of production, they will become soulless "hands," to whom life is a matter of doing as little work as possible and then escaping into the illusion of happiness and pride through vice.

Therefore, in order to fulfill its own purpose of bringing men to God, the Church must seek to ensure that men can have dignity in their lives and in their work. It must itself become a force of social justice and it must work with other forces of social justice wherever they are, and whatever they are called. Further, the Church must recognize that men can only progress and can only grow in dignity by working for themselves, and working together for their common good. The Church cannot uplift a man; it can only help to provide the conditions and the opportunity for him to cooperate with his fellows to uplift himself.

Cooperation with Non-Christians

It is not necessary to agree with everything a man believes, or says, in order to work with him on particular projects or in particular areas of activity. The Church must stand up for what it believes to be right; that is its justification and purpose. But it should welcome all who stand on the same side, and continue regardless of which individuals or groups it is then opposing.

A good does not become evil if a Communist says it is a good; an evil does not become good if a Fascist supports it. Exploiting the poor does not become a right thing to do because Communists call it a wrong thing; production for profit rather than meeting human needs does not become more just because Communists say it leads to injustice. Organizing the society in such a manner that people live together and work together for their common good does not become an evil because it is called socialism. A system based on greed and selfishness does not become good because it is labelled free enterprise. Let the Church choose for itself what is right and what is wrong in accordance with Christian principles, and let it not be affected by what other groups or individuals do or say. But let it welcome cooperation from all those who agree with its judgments.

We know that we are fallible men and that our task is to serve, not to judge. Yet we accept into the Church (provided only that they come to mass every Sunday and pay their dues or contribute to missionary activities) those who create and maintain the present political and economic system. But it is this system which has led to millions being hungry, thirsty, and naked; it is this system which makes men strangers in their own countries because they are poor, powerless, and oppressed; it is this system which condemns millions to preventable sickness, and which makes prisoners of men who have the courage to protest. What right, then, have we to reject those who serve mankind, simply because they refuse to accept the leadership of the Church, or refuse to acknowledge the divinity of Jesus or the existence of God? What right have we to presume that God Almighty takes no notice of those who give dedicated services to those millions of His children who hunger and thirst after justice, just because they do not do it in His Name? If God were to ask the wretched of the earth who are their friends, are we so sure that we know their answer? And is that answer irrelevant to those who seek to serve God?

The Role of the Church

What all this amounts to is a call to the Church to recognize the need for social revolution, and to play a leading role in it. For it is a fact of history that almost all the successful social revolutions which have taken place in the world have been led by people who were themselves beneficiaries under the system they sought to replace. Time and again members of the privileged classes have joined, and often led, the poor or oppressed in their revolts against injustice. The same things must happen now.

Within the rich countries of the world the beneficiaries of educational opportunity, of good health, and of security must be prepared to stand up and demand justice for those who have up to now been denied these things. Where the poor have already begun to demand a just society, at least some members of the privileged classes must help them and encourage them. Where they have not begun to do so, it is the responsibility of those who have had greater opportunities for development to arouse the poor out of their poverty-induced apathy. And I am saying that Christians should be prominent among those who do this, and that the Church should seek to increase the numbers and the power of those who refuse to acquiesce in established injustices.

Only by its activity in these fields can the Church justify its relevance in the modern world. For the purpose of the Church is Man—his human dignity, and his right to develop himself in freedom. To the service of Man's development, any or all of the institutions of any particular society must be sacrificed if this should be necessary. For all human institutions, including the Church, are established in order to serve Man. And it is the institution of the Church, through its members, which should be leading the attack on any organization, or any economic, social, or political structure which oppresses men, and which denies to them the right and power to live as the sons of a loving God.

In the poor countries the Church has this same role to play. It has to be consistently and actively on the side of the poor and unprivileged. It has to lead men towards Godliness by joining with them in the attack against the injustices and deprivation from which they suffer. It must cooperate with all those who are involved in this work; it must reject alliances with those who represent Mammon, and cooperate with all those who are working for Man. Its members must go out as servants of the world, as men and women who wish to share their knowledge and their abilities with those whom they recognize as their brothers and their sisters in Christ. . . .

SOURCE: Julius K. Nyerere, "On the Division Between Rich and Poor," in *Moral Issues and Christian Response,* ed. Paul T. Jersild (New York: Holt, Rinehart and Winston, 1976), pp. 237–243.

VI
Relationship with Self

Introduction

"To get my own head together" is an ominous-sounding task to many in this age. It can also be a selfish task, if it is pursued directly, as a top priority, with all other needs and interests subordinated to it.

For the Christian, "getting myself together" is a by-product rather than a direct goal. If a Christian is in loving union with God through Christ, in unselfish loving relationships with one's brothers and sisters, and has a thoughtful and reverent response to the physical world, then there can be no other condition of the "self" than one of sound integration and fullness of experience. How else could the "inner self" be than peaceful, if one is at peace with all the rest of reality?

"To get my own head together" is a relational happening, not a self-contained one. It does not occur because we have pursued it relentlessly. It comes because we have understood well that there is a "place for everything" in God's creation.

Much Christian spirituality in the past six hundred years (since the time of the brilliant philosopher-theologians of the twelfth and thirteenth centuries) seems to have suggested that the primary task in life was to mold a perfect Christian personality within oneself. One got the feeling of being in the role of a sculptor who had been given a choice piece of marble by the Creator. A person would be held accountable by God for chiselling this choice bit of raw material into a perfect finished product. To be able to present a finely-polished masterpiece to the original Gift-giver at the end of life would be ultimate success.

That is a warped notion of Christian purpose. God does not set each of us to the task of perfecting a "raw human nature" in our life span of twenty or fifty or ninety years. That's a self-centered way of looking at Christianity. It leads us to stare at self constantly, to measure our spiritual development on "growth charts," on "data sheets."

151

If we got angry twenty times last month and did so only ten times this month, then we must be getting holier!

Such self-analysis and self-measurement can easily lead to self-exaltation, inane vanity, perhaps even to self-destruction. Why self-destruction? Very much like a laser beam, or any firing weapon, if you turn it in on itself, its own force destroys itself. If you reflect the brilliant rays of the sun on an object outside self, you can see the object all the more clearly. If you reflect those same rays into your own eyes, you burn them up in an instant.

This does not mean at all that Christianity is not interested in the perfect development of each individual person. Just the opposite, Christianity wishes to see each human person develop his or her talents to the utmost. It means simply that Christianity does not teach self-perfection as an end-in-itself. The perfect human being, the one who is happy with self, the one who loves self thoroughly, is the person who strives to be at peace with God, with other human beings, with the totality of the physical world.

In this consists the true love of self. "You shall love your neighbor as yourself." Indeed, God has singled out love of self as the guide for love of others. Yet many of us go through life without loving and accepting ourselves as fully as we might—perhaps because we do not really know ourselves. We do not fully realize that there is nobody like me—like you. Each of us is unique, special, unrepeatable . . . with both limitations and talents. In the Old Testament, this theme of self-knowledge is found in the Psalms (e.g., Psalm 118:59) and it is prominent in the Wisdom literature.

Through the internal journey of meditation, for example, we can begin to know ourselves, our abilities, to care about ourselves, to share ourselves. You may, for example, be one of the world's greatest winkers, capable of bringing joy to many people with your wink. But if you don't know this and appreciate that ability, all that wonderful joy may never be realized. Perfecting self is a by-product of knowing and sharing that ability.

The committed Christian concentrates on being open to all reality, and especially to the ultimate reality, God, confident of God's supportive presence in all of the ordinary events and tasks of daily living. When we achieve this, there is a great lessening of the frustration that comes from our human limitations.

It is true that, in the light of the divine presence, we may see more clearly than ever before how our limited human condition is incapable of bringing to completion our own yearnings. But this awareness is no longer a bother! Finite human creatures find a certain contentment in experiencing divine presence in the here and now, a divine presence that begins to quench our straining for infinity.

The ideal relationship with self in Christianity comes from a calm acceptance and development of our unique talents, from an intense effort to relate those talents well to all the rest of reality. Christian self-perfection can never be grasped; in a strict sense, it cannot be achieved by our direct efforts. Rather, it is happening when we relate well to our brothers and sisters, to material creation, to our Creator.

22

Sin as Unrelatedness

Andre-Marie Dubarle

A little over fifteen hundred years ago, an Italian theologian named Julian asked St. Augustine this famous question in their controversy over original sin: "How can two baptized parents pass on what they themselves no longer have?" If baptism really takes away original sin, how can baptized parents literally pass on what has been washed away from their souls?

Augustine's answer, and the responses of numerous medieval Christian theologians, has been neither clear nor satisfying. Perhaps the simplest indication of their unsatisfactoriness is—how many readers of this book, schooled in the Christian faith, can readily answer the question of Julian?

Andre-Marie Dubarle gives a clear, direct and scriptural answer to this centuries-old question in the following selection from his book, *The Biblical Doctrine of Original Sin.* Dubarle does not bend over backward, as some modern theologians do, and suggest that there has been no real content to the traditional Christian teaching of original sin. Rather, he says very directly that the great problem in our traditional teaching was to conceive of the transmission of original sin as the passing on of an "internal stain" or blemish on the soul, much as parents might pass on a chronic kidney condition to their children. In the "sin of the world" theory which he presents, original sin is transmitted simply by the fact that a child is born into a world of broken relationships—broken relationships with God and with other human beings. Just as a child could not be born in New York City and be untouched by decades of air pollution, so a child cannot be born into the human condition untouched by centuries of sinfulness.

In his explanation of original sin, Dubarle gives a fine sense of what sin is in general. Sin is not a thing. Sin is not guilt. Sin is not a broken law. Sin *is* a broken relationship. God offers his friendship, takes the initiative to be united to us, and we reject or at least "mess up" the union. (Not only is sin a broken relationship with God, but it can be properly conceived of as a breaking of any of the four basic relationships.)

We include this discussion of sin under the general heading of "relationship to self" in this book (although it could fit under any of the other three) in order to correct an imbalance in our traditional way of looking at sin. Too many Christians have been taught that a certain action, a certain thought, a certain attitude is sinful because some religious authority has declared it so. This leads to a rather impersonal notion of sin and virtue, to a concept of virtue as a "satisfied rule-keeping." Sin becomes a matter of being caught breaking the rules.

Rather, sin is its own punishment. Sin destroys our own integrity. Sin causes us to be poorly-related human beings. Sin leaves us creatures of miserable imbalance. Sin thwarts us from enjoying that fullness that comes from being well-related to those three; there is no hope that we can be at peace with ourselves.

Andre-Marie Dubarle is a prominent European scholar with a primary expertise in the Old Testament. He is professor of Sacred Scripture at the Dominican House of Studies of Le Saulchoir in France. His *Biblical Doctrine of Original Sin* is considered by many modern theologians to be the best summary to date of contemporary thought on the subject of original sin.

Original sin is not a unique catastrophe at the birth of our species; it is the continually perpetuated perversion of mankind, in which new sins are conditioned more or less by the preceding sins and carry on the existing disorder. Instead of a disturbance that would die away in three or four generations, there is a generalized and anonymous corruption, with everyone its victim and many its authors, but in such a way that more often than not it is impossible to pinpoint any individual responsibility. In the story of the Tower of Babel (Gen. 11:1–9) one of these collective faults is shown bringing in its train dire consequences, which remain for later generations. It is easy to see that this passage involves a great deal of generalization and simplification, when it reduces to one localized event a number of facts leading to the divergence of language and opposition between peoples. The question is whether it is unfaithful to the intention of the inspired author, or whether the teaching of St. Paul is gravely compromised, if we admit an analogous literary genre in Chapter 3 of the same book.

St. Augustine was struck by the Bible texts that told of ancestors being punished in their posterity and he put forward a theory that theologians have sometimes considered strange, but that could still be very stimulating. In his eyes original sin is modified in each generation by the merits or demerits of individuals; parents increase or lessen for their children the burden of penalty and sin, which is passed on by the act of generation. Compared with the catastrophic corruption brought on by the fault of our first father these additions or subtractions remain relatively unimportant and original sin is not gradually obliterated in a long line of just men. Only the grace of Christ can succeed in remitting it entirely. These ideas, when compared with the questions being asked by modern literary criticism, can help in forming the concept of a universal state of original sin, but one that proceeds from multiple sources. This leaves room for a certain individual variability, although the main common features are present everywhere.

What we suffer from is not only the fault of a distant ancestor but as much and above all far closer sins, which in their turn were provoked by earlier sins. We could speak today of a chain reaction and such an idea seems to us to fit in with what we see elsewhere of mankind's condition. Each of us, because he is born into a world and a race contaminated by sin, is born a sinner. 'That which is born of the flesh is flesh' (John 3:6). He cannot enter the kingdom of God without first being cleansed.

Many modern exegetes refuse to see in the story of the Fall the story of an individual event. In their eyes it is only a kind of parable, illustrating the universal fact of sin in mankind. From the point of view of literary criticism such an interpretation is far from unfounded. But what it ignores or overlooks, what catholic dogma proclaims with insistence and teaches us not to add to the text but to recognize in it, is the fact that sin like all other elements of man's destiny is not a strictly individual matter. Its consequences weigh heavy on the posterity of the culprits. In the case of a man and his wife it is the whole of mankind that is now in the grip of fear at God's approach, banished far from the garden of happiness, condemned to death and the penalty of work by the sweat of the brow. Underlying the text is the idea of a heritage of sin.

Between the interpretation of many modern exegetes, who see in Chapter 3 of Genesis only the stylized outline of individual sin, and the early and usual interpretation, which sees in it the account of a particular sin at the beginning which had consequences for the whole of mankind, there is room for an intermediate position, admitting the schematic and universal nature of the narrative but not missing the main point, a sin handed on by inheritance: what the text describes is the effect of a countless multitude of individual sins.

Perhaps a faithful catholic is not today in a position to provide unanswerable arguments in support of this interpretation. Perhaps the positive science of human origins, which at the moment is unable to affirm the existence of a single couple, the ancestors of all men, will one day succeed in finally rejecting this or incontrovertibly proving it. Perhaps the theologians will agree to accept the idea offered them by biblical exegesis: the idea of a symbolic and schematic account, intending to describe not a strictly individual event but a universal condition passed on by inheritance. Perhaps on the other hand they will succeed in showing that strict unity of physical origin is so necessarily bound up with the universality of original sin that the first cannot be denied without the second being abandoned. It is not always easy to discover at the outset the remote consequences of a new idea, nor is it easy to form a complete picture of all the internal connections of revealed truths and so estimate the repercussions of a denial that may at first seem unobjectionable.

. . . We can, in conformity with the suggestions of the evolution theory, admit that mankind emerged from the animal world. Leaving aside the existence of a spiritual soul, the transition may have been very gradual. In the case of the soul, which either does or does not exist, there can have been no gradual transition, although all its rich potential would not have been immediately manifest to external observation: Man began gradually to diverge from the animals in his way of life, while sin began to form that heritage of perversion that was handed on at the same time as the heritage of technical culture.

Such a theory, attempting to do justice to the evidence of our modern knowledge of human origins as well as to the biblical data taken as a whole and not just the two solitary texts of Genesis 3 and Romans 5, does not compromise the gravity of original sin. Instead of concentrating on the loss of wonderful and gratuitous gifts, whose disappearance does not really injure our nature in itself, this theory fixes its attention on quite concrete troubles we find in our actual experience and that the Genesis narrative represented in a stylized way: a poisoning of our trusting relationship with God and various sufferings. The doctrine of original sin consists in stating that not everything that worries us can be explained by the still incomplete development of man's spiritual powers or by the failures of an evolutive system that would leave room for mistakes or a process of trial and error on man's own level as well as on the level of the formation of the species. In the present state of humanity there is a disorder (not just something missing) on the religious as well as the human level, and this is the result of deliberate sin. Individuals are embroiled in this disorder whether they like it or not: and it is of small importance whether the point of departure was close to the animal state, as modern evolution theory thinks, or raised far above it, as was thought for a long time by theologians who did not have the information that we possess today. The essential point is that the present state of mankind, with the baneful influence that it exercises on newcomers to existence, is the result of deliberate faults and that even the initial religious state of young children is vitiated by it. . . .

We see original sin now as a truly tragic and actual situation: no longer merely the loss of wonderful gifts at a great remove from our day and condition, but the moral and religious perversion in which every man finds himself inevitably plunged by reason of his birth into a perverted environment: ignorance of God, or idolatry and a more or less profound corruption.

Mankind is oppressed by a countless mass of sins: it is impossible accurately to pinpoint the individual responsibility for this. In each generation the harmfulness of this distant downfall is reactivated by new sins. And the pressure of the social environment forces some of this corruption into the empty souls of children, just as physical heredity transmits blemishes or some lack of balance. Nobody can claim to have escaped this condition: everyone needs a Saviour.

The grace of Christianity now appears not only as a free gift, giving something better than what went before, but also as the pardon of a condemned prisoner, the salvation of something that was lost. 'Save yourselves from this crooked generation' (Acts 2:40) 'You know that you were ransomed from the futile ways inherited from your fathers, not with perishable things such as silver or gold, but with the precious blood of Christ, like that of a lamb without blemish or spot' (1 Peter 1:18–19).

SOURCE: Andre-Marie Dubarle, *The Biblical Doctrine of Original Sin* (New York: Herder and Herder, 1964), pp. 224–226, 236–237, 244–245.

23
Conscience
Charles Curran

"Follow your conscience" is the battle cry for the liberated person of the twentieth-century Western world. It would seem reasonable to presume, then, that the person who echoes this cry as he or she plunges into moral decision-making should have an accurate idea of what conscience is.

That's not an easy task. As Charles Curran points out in the following selection, theologians, Church councils, and even the writers of Christian Scripture have disagreed on what the determining characteristics of conscience are, at various intervals in the history of Christianity. There still does not seem to be one universally agreed upon description of this elusive agent which almost all people turn to in order to justify their moral (or immoral) activities.

Is conscience a distinct faculty within the make-up of the human person? Is it merely the conscious mind intelligently at work on a moral problem? Is it simply the way one feels about the morality of an action? Is it God within a person giving some direction about morality?

Most authors, and Curran is no exception, conclude that moral conscience is a combination of certain of the above characteristics. In what he calls a "synthetic approach," Curran defines conscience as a concrete judgment of practical reason (i.e., reason at work on an action that the person must do here and now) about the moral goodness of a particular act, made under the influence of synteresis (i.e., an intuitive sense of right and wrong that is within us all). It is accurate to conclude that, in Curran's view, conscience is not a separate faculty inside a person. It is not a mechanism, complete within itself, that exists independently of the mind. It is the mind at work, but specifically at work on a here-and-now moral decision, under the influence of that intuitive sense of what is right and wrong.

In this view, conscience does not make generalizations such as "Birth control is right" or "Abortion is wrong." Since it is defined as a judgment of the *practical reason,* it is concerned only with the morality of the immediate action to be done by the one deciding. It is the competency of conscience to state, "It is moral/immoral for me to undergo this abortion now." It is moral science that gives us principles and generalizations, not conscience.

One should note carefully that conscience works on a moral decision for the personal actions of the one deciding. It is inaccurate to speak of "*my* conscience telling *me* that *you* should . . ." We advise others with our moral wisdom and intelligence, with the fruits of experience, not with conscience.

However, the Christian must never lose sight of the fact that, although conscience is at work only at the moment of a personal decision, it is always possible to prepare conscience for that moment. A maturing moral knowledge, the advice of wise mentors, the unfolding understanding of revelation under the guidance of the Spirit—all work together to ready conscience for the critical moment of its practical judgment. Conscience is not the solitary court of appeal for morality; it is, rather, the *final* court of appeal.

It is interesting to note that Curran places little emphasis on the "voice of God" within as an ingredient of conscience. Traditionally Christian theologians have maintained that every human being, made in the image of God, has within self a divine reflection that guides one to sound moral decision-making, almost as though it were a separate agent within the person speaking to that individual. This facet was so prominent in the Christian tradition that many people still accept the following manner of speaking, "My conscience tells me," or, "My conscience bothers me," as though the "me" and "conscience" could be distinguished. Perhaps modern psychology, with its analysis of the "id" and subconscious, has caused contemporary theologians to tread lightly on the issue of the "God within".

Charles Curran is professor of moral theology at The

Catholic University of America in Washington, D.C. He is one of the most popular and best known of American Catholic moral theologians, and has written extensively in the area of contemporary moral issues. Perhaps his best-known work is *Christian Morality Today*, from which this selection has been taken.

Even a superficial reflection shows the existence of moral conscience. Man experiences the joy of having done good or the remorse of having done evil. He recognizes an imperative to do this or avoid that. A more profound analysis distinguishes moral conscience from social pressure or even a religious imperative.

Moral conscience has many meanings. St. Paul describes conscience as a witness or judge of past activity, a director of future action, the habitual quality of a man's Christianity, and even as the Christian ego or personality. This chapter will discuss the problem of antecedent conscience; that is, conscience as pointing out to the Christian what he should do in the particular circumstances of his life.

Historical Summary

Scripture reveals Christianity as a dialogue or covenant relationship between God and his people. Christian tradition frequently refers to conscience as the voice of God telling man how to respond to the divine gift of salvation. Both the reality and the concept of moral conscience have evolved in the course of salvation history. Two reasons explain the evolution. First, God speaks to primitive man in one way and to more mature man in another way. Second, only when man has acquired a certain degree of maturity can he reflect on his own subjective states.

In the beginning of salvation history, conscience (the reality, not the word) appears as extrinsic, objective, and collective. Theophany, however, gives way to angelophany, and finally to human prophets who speak in the name of God. The prophets, the conscience of Israel, stress interior dispositions and begin to mention individual responsibility (Jer 31:29–30; Ez 14:1–8). They look forward to the day when God will plant his law in the innermost part of man (Jer 31:33–34; Ez 36:26–27: Psalm 50:12). Since the prophets insist on God as the first cause, conscience is not the voice of man but the voice of God who speaks to man.

St. Paul, with his emphasis on the internal and subjective dispositions of man, brings into Christian thought the term conscience which originally appeared in Democritus and was developed by stoic philosophy. Paul, while adopting the uses of the term in pagan philosophy, introduces the notion of conscience as the director of human activity—antecedent conscience. Commenting on the different Pauline uses of the term conscience, the Fathers of the Church explicitly make the last step in the interiorization of conscience. Conscience now becomes the voice of the human person himself and only mediately and indirectly the voice of God.

Scholastic theology of the thirteenth century first considered scientifically, as opposed to the pastoral approach of the Fathers, the nature of moral conscience. Is it a faculty? A habit? An act? The Thomistic school distinguished conscience, the judgment of the practical reason about a particular act, from synteresis, the quasi-innate habit of the first principles of the moral order. St. Bonaventure placed more emphasis on the will, especially with regard to synteresis. The subjective voice of reason was open to God through the mediation of law.

Unfortunately, the scholastic synthesis succumbed to the dangers of sterile intellectualism, the nominalistic tendency to extrinsicism, and the increasing influence of positive juridic sciences. The decree of the Council of Trent again legislating the necessity of annual confession of sins according to their number and species orientated moral theology (and the question of conscience) toward the judgment seat of the confessional rather than toward the living of the Christian life.

The Nature of Conscience

Guided by the lessons of history, one can better understand the nature of conscience, its function, and its formation. Catholic theologians generally distinguish synteresis, moral science, and conscience. Adopting a synthetic approach, we can define synteresis as the power of conscience situated in the inmost part of the soul (scintilla animae). In its rational aspect, synteresis tends to the truth so that man almost intuitively knows the fundamental principle of the moral order—good is to be done and evil is to be avoided. In its volitional aspect, synteresis tends toward the good and the expression of such a tendency in action.

Moral science is the knowledge of the less general principles of the moral law which man deduces from the primary principles. The category of moral knowledge also includes whatever man knows from revelation or authority. It pertains to the objective, the conceptual, the essential order.

Conscience is the concrete judgment of the practical reason, made under the twofold influence of synteresis, about the moral goodness of a particular act. Conscience forms its judgment discursively from the objective principles of the moral order; but at the same time, there is also a direct con-natural knowing process. The dictate of conscience is concrete, subjective, individual, and existential.

Conscience tells man what he should do. Man's "ought" follows from his "is." Man's actions must affirm his being. St. Paul makes Christian existence the foundation of Christian morality. The Christian is baptized into the death and resurrection of Christ. Consequently, he must die to self and walk in the newness of life (Rom 6). Man's existence is a loving dependence on his God and a communion with his fellow men. Human endeavor must express this twofold personal relationship.

Conscience and human freedom are not completely autonomous. In practice man rejects the complete autonomy of conscience. In the eyes of the world Adolf Eichmann and the Nazis were guilty of crimes against humanity despite the plea of a clear conscience. Conscience must act in accord with the nature and person of man. The greatest possible freedom and the greatest possible happiness for man consist in the fulfillment of his own being.

The judgment of conscience expresses with regard to a particular act the fundamental tendency of man to truth and good. The basis of Christian morality, however, is not man's relation to an abstract principle, but to a person, God. Since he first loved us, God has freely given us his love, his friendship, our salvation. Scripture uses the words faith and love to express man's acceptance and response to God's gift. Like Christ himself, man's external actions must manifest this love. At the same time man's actions dispose him to enter more intimately into the mystery of divine love. The ultimate norm of Christian conduct is this: what does the love of God demand of me in these concrete circumstances? Love, as a complete giving of self and not a mere emotion, seeks always the will of the beloved.

The Formation of Conscience

God speaks to us through the very existence he has given us—creation, salvation, our talents, abilities and even weaknesses, and the existential circumstances of our situation. In other words, the will of the beloved is made known to us through his "laws"—the law of the Spirit, the natural law, positive law, and the law of the situation.

The primary law of the new covenant is the internal law of the Spirit, the law of Christ, the law of love. Even Christ, however, found it necessary to express his law in external rules; but the demands are comparatively general; e.g., the beatitudes.

God also speaks to man through the human nature he has given him. The natural law, as theologians call it, is primarily a dynamic, internal law. Since it is the very law of man's existence and being, it has an absolute character. Christ, at least implicitly, affirmed the value of the natural law within the framework of the new covenant. The law of nature is assumed into the law of Christ, for all nature was created according to the image of Christ and all nature exists for Christ. From the first principle of the natural law, more objective, detailed rules of conduct are formulated.

Unfortunately, many Catholic theologians have exaggerated the natural law. It is not the primary law for the Christian. Some have succumbed to the temptation of using the natural law as a club. Others have overextended it in attempting to prove the moral certitude of mere hypotheses. Many still tend to codify completely the natural law and thus rob the natural law of its dynamic character.

Living in human society, the Christian is also the subject of human law, both civil and ecclesiastical. Such law is purely external and consequently seen as an infringement of human liberty. Since positive legislation is not absolute, it does not oblige when in conflict with the interest of the higher laws.

God has called each person by his own name. In one sense, every individual is unique; every concrete situation is unique. The Christian's answer to the divine call must correspond to his individual circumstances.

Conscience is a supernaturally elevated subjective power of man. The law of Christ and the natural law are primarily internal laws. Why then is it necessary to have detailed, particular, external expressions of these laws? Why a code? Man's love of God is not yet perfect. Fallen human nature still experiences the tendency to self and not to God. Spiritual schizophrenia is a necessary characteristic of earthly Christianity. Even the impulsive reaction of the human will of Christ was to avoid the sacrifice willed by his Father. Love of God is by its nature a self-sacrificing love. Man in his present state cannot know perfectly what the demands of love of God are. Particular, external expressions of the law of love and natural law have a value only insofar as they point out the minimum and basic demands of the law of love. Code morality is not opposed to an ethic of love.

External law, if considered without any relation to the internal law, can be even an occasion of sin (Gal 3:19; Rom 5:20–21; 7:5–23). The external law is static and very incomplete. It does not and cannot express the totality of man's relationship to God. The vast majority of the decisions of conscience pertain to matters where there are no determined external expressions of law. Thus far we have not been speaking of the positive human laws which are primarily external. Here, too, self-sacrificing love of God and respect for the common good move man to obey positive law despite its inherent imperfections, unless such positive law runs counter to a higher law.

The formation and training of conscience include much more than the mere knowledge of external formulas of law. Insistence on external law is the haven of the insecure (neuroticism, scrupulosity) or the shallow (legalism, Phariseeism). Christian morality is ultimately love, an "I-thou" relationship between God and man. By meditation on true values, the Christian grows in wisdom and age and grace. Likewise, the formation of conscience must take into consideration the findings of many of the positive sciences. For example, what purports to be religious obedience might in reality be the manifestation of an inferiority complex. A proper formation, joined with the virtue of prudence acquired in daily Christian experiences, prepares the conscience to hear the call of God's love.

Space permits the mention of only two important characteristics of Christian conscience: communitarian and creative. A communitarian conscience recognizes man's relationship with his fellow men in the kingdom of God. A communitarian conscience avoids excessive individualism and the opposite extreme of mass hypnosis. A creative conscience, attuned to the Spirit, throws off the shackles of stultifying legalism. A true Christian conscience leads man to make Christianity and Christian love "the light of the world and the salt of the earth"—a positive commitment to the kingdom of God in its reality both as the city of God and the city of man.

Reality is complex. The problems of conscience are complex. Frequently, there are no easy solutions. After prayerful consideration of all values involved, the Christian chooses what he believes to be the demands of love in the present situation. The Christian can never expect to have perfect, mathematical certitude about his actions. The virtue of humility preserves him from falling into the opposed extremes of introspective anxiety and mere formalism.

Neurotic anxiety has no place in Christianity. Christianity is fundamentally a religion of joy—of man's participation in the joy and triumph of the resurrection. The paradox of Christianity is that joy comes through self-sacrificing love.

For the Christian who has made a commensurate effort to form his conscience correctly, the dictate of conscience is an infallible norm of conduct. Even though the action itself is not in objective conformity with the divine will, the Christian's conduct is pleasing to God, for it stems from a pure heart.

SOURCE: Charles Curran, *Christian Morality Today* (Notre Dame, Indiana: Fides, 1966), pp. 13–15, 17–22.

24
Freedom
John F. O'Grady

John F. O'Grady is director of continuing education for Catholic clergy in the diocese of Albany. He is the author of two books: *Jesus, Lord and Christ* and *Christian Anthropology: A Meaning for Human Life,* from which this selection on freedom is taken.

The word "freedom" has several meanings: lack of physical restraint, absence of external social pressure or of internal neurosis. Sometimes, unfortunately, freedom is associated with arbitrary license. There is, however, a much more profound and subtle meaning of freedom.

Though freedom is relative, it nonetheless implies that we are able to act without ultimately compelling influences, but on the basis of our own insights and choices. We presuppose that the human person has prior reasons or motives impelling to action. But action which is motivated is not action which is necessarily unfree. It is *conditioned* but not *forced.* Freedom consists in the ability to choose which motives are to guide action. Freedom, therefore, is the state in which we are able to create our lives through our choices.

Choice: here lies a great difficulty in life—not so much in the choice between good and evil, but in the choice between good and good. A young girl, for example, may vacillate among a dozen possible satisfying and worthwhile professions, but for the mature woman choices *must* be made. Freedom of choice is an opportunity, a challenge, a responsibility, and, at times, a burden. In its most fundamental sense freedom, according to O'Grady, is "the ability to commit oneself to an ideal, to actively give oneself over to the fullness of reality and thereby achieve liberating and peace-giving effects."

With this background, we can now speak about freedom of the Christian. First of all, Christian freedom is freedom from any radical anxiety about ourselves. Jesus stated:

> I tell you not to worry about the food you need to stay alive or about the clothes you need for your body. . . . Your Father knows you need these things. Instead be concerned with his Kingdom, and he will provide you with these things (Luke 12:22, 30–31).

Because Christians are fundamentally free *from* radical anxiety about self, they can be all the more free *for* participation in building God's kingdom by reaching out in sensitive understanding and active caring for fellow human beings.

> Remember that you have been called to live in freedom. . . . Out of love, place yourselves at one another's service. The whole law has found its fulfillment in this one saying: "You shall love your neighbor as yourself" (Gal. 5:13–14).

Insofar as this type of freedom is actually being lived, one is thereby reaching out not only to other human persons, but also to God and to one's own Christian personhood, as described in the Last Judgment depiction of Matthew 25. Christians believe that such a free person is beyond the control of—and slavery to—sin and death. Such a person is truly free.

Freedom

. . . Modern man is still discovering the implications of human freedom. The very confusion in the meaning of the word testifies to that. The French Revolution may have liberated man from the *ancien régime*; psychology may have liberated man from servitude to instincts, modern technology may have freed him from drudgery, but the constant call for freedom NOW from political, social, psychological, and even religious quarters gives ample proof that freedom is still to come.

The challenging feature of modern times is freedom and its possibilities. In spite of the French and American revolutions, we still suffer from the evils of capitalistic liberalism and totalitarianism. We are threatened by the abuse of psychology and the disintegrating effects of analysis and sensitivity sessions. Automation may eventually enslave man to the machine. Even within Christianity we have still to learn what it means to live in the royal freedom of Jesus Christ. There is an urgent need to understand more accurately the meaning of freedom.

Almost everyone knows what freedom means: freedom is the capacity to act or not to act, to do this or to do that. Precisely because everyone knows this description of freedom, the meaning of freedom is misunderstood. This is really a very superficial image of freedom. According to this image, freedom is a neutral power by which every person at any given moment is capable of picking out from an infinite variety of possible actions, whether good or bad, heroic or petty, the one that suits his fancy. This is wrong. A man is never free to do exactly what he wants at every moment of his life. Our lives are conditioned by environment, heredity, and education. We are not the totally free people we pretend to be. The image is wrong on a more fundamental level. True freedom involves the whole person and is not a neutral but a positive act. Freedom in its most fundamental sense is the ability to commit oneself to an ideal, to actively give oneself over to the fullness of reality and thereby achieve liberating and peace-giving effects.

From the depths of one's creativity, every person must commit himself to outside reality as a whole. This is a fundamental choice between love and selfishness, between ego-centeredness and thou-centeredness. The person either radically agrees to the whole, the fullness of reality outside himself in a spirit of openness, service, respect, and love, or he radically refers everything to himself. Freedom is the ability a person has to reject or accept God. The freedom of choice, to do this or that, is not worthy of consideration in the presence of the true and ultimate freedom of the acceptance or rejection of God.

Freedom in Scripture

The Gospels present Jesus of Nazareth as a free man. Jesus knew and loved the traditions of his ancestors; he respected the Sabbath but always within bounds. He cured on the Sabbath (Luke 6:7), allowed his disciples to pick grain on the Sabbath (Luke 6:1). He fulfilled the demands of the law when the law helped people, but would not worry about eating with unclean hands, especially when people fulfilled this prescription but left their hearts unclean (Matt. 7:1–23). He accepted social customs and told the leper to show himself to the High Priest (Luke 5:12–14), but broke social customs when they were inhuman. He gladly spoke to sinners and ate with publicans (Luke 5:30). For Jesus, the law was the expression of the love of God and neighbor:

> This is the greatest and first commandment. The second is like it: "You shall love your neighbor as yourself." On these two commandments the whole law is based, and the prophets as well. (Matt. 22:38–40)

This was his basic law with every situation and interpretation founded on the love of God and neighbor. Jesus was free in regard to law and social custom because he interpreted the law in light of the love of God and neighbor.

The Gospels present Jesus as the man who was free because he had given himself to his Father, had actively disposed of himself in the presence of the fullness of reality that is his Father, and with all of his being committed his life and eventually his death to the will of his Father. Jesus was free because he loved God and loved men.

The second spokesman for freedom in the New Testament is Paul. He developed Christian freedom in terms of freedom from sin, from law and death. What Jesus had manifested in his life was now possible for the lives of believers if they accepted the royal freedom of their Master.

Freedom from sin is the heart of the redemption as accomplished in Jesus. This is freedom from the state of estrangement from God and freedom from the wrath of God that man had merited. Paul knows that for the believer sin and evil will not prevail; the power of sin is broken and man is now under the more powerful influence of good, but only if man accepts the offer (Rom. 6:1–4, 14, 20–23).

The second expression of freedom is freedom from law. The law for Paul is good in itself, but it had never given man the strength to avoid sin. With its commandments and prohibitions it had succeeded in giving man an appetite for sin. Law brought sin into experience. With Jesus, man is no longer bound to the law since he is beyond the law with the presence of the Spirit (Rom. 7:4–11; Gal. 2:4; 4:21–31; 5:1–15). The relationship between law and spirit is treated by Paul in the seventh and eighth chapters of Romans. The basic conclusion reached by Paul is that the Christian needs no law as long as he lives the life of the Spirit. There is no place for legalism in Christianity. Christian man is to live by the Spirit.

The third freedom is freedom from death, which for Paul is always a consequence of sin. Paul speaks of eternal death since only then would sin claim its decisive victory (Rom. 6:8; 1 Cor. 15:20–22, 55–57).

This threefold freedom from sin, law, and death is realized in three stages. Fundamentally it comes from the cross of Jesus. Through his act of obedience and his death, he won freedom for us. The sign of Christian freedom is the sign of the cross of Jesus (Rom. 6:6–7). This freedom becomes a reality for us inasmuch as it is offered to us as a call from God.

> My brothers, remember that you have been called to live in freedom—but not a freedom that gives free rein to the flesh. Out of love, place yourselves at one another's service. (Gal. 5:13)

We become free when we accept the gift of God as seen in the life, death, and resurrection of Jesus. Christian existence is a constant call to freedom from sin, law, and death, begun in baptism.

Paul's third stage is to live in love: "Since we live by the Spirit, let us follow the Spirit's lead" (Gal. 5:25). The new law of love fulfills our call to freedom as we learn to bear one another's failings (Gal. 6:2). Full freedom is what Paul expresses to the Galatians:

> The life I live now is not my own; Christ is living in me. I still live my human life, but it is a life of faith in the Son of God, who loved me and gave himself for me. (Gal. 2:20)

Finally, in Paul we must see that Christian freedom is never complete until the experience of death. The final freedom is the freedom of the sons of God when we will share in the glory of God, through the sharings of his life. Scripture sees freedom as the ability of man to dispose himself to the love of God that is perfected in death, but present in the expressions of the love of neighbor. We are free from sin and law and death, which was begun for us in Jesus Christ and his death, and is offered to us as a call. Freedom is the ability to accept or reject God through the acceptance or rejection of the neighbor in life and in death, which will sum up what was previously expressed in life.

Theology of Freedom

When the Word became flesh we reached the highest point of the self-realization of human freedom. By this act a man was called and responded to give himself completely to the mystery that is God. In the incarnation, a human being was called to communicate with God to the greatest depths of possibility, and this human being responded in freedom in the life that he lived and the human death that he accepted. The Word became man and fulfilled the possibilities of human freedom. The life and death of Jesus of Nazareth explains the possibility of human freedom.

The freedom of Jesus was possible because man is spirit in the world, able to transcend the possibilities of his space and time and enter into communion with his God. Human transcendence is directed to the mystery of God because God has so created man with an orientation and a possibility for communion with himself. The conclusion of such thinking is that God, as the foundation for transcendence and for freedom, is willed in every act of freedom, whether this is conscious or not. Man is not forced to accept his transcendence; there is always the possibility of consent or refusal and it is this possibility that constitutes his freedom. The Christian theology of freedom always relates man and his transcendence to God.

To speak of freedom as directed toward God does not imply, however, that freedom is divorced from this world. Freedom always presupposes the object that is in the world. Even the most profound acceptance of God in freedom is mediated in creation. We meet God in the most radical way everywhere and in the most powerful way in the presence of the neighbor. The free man is one like Jesus Christ who has given himself to his God through the giving of himself to others.

Finally, freedom is a trustful creative task that is given at every interval of life. It is trustful because it calls man to give up himself in order to find himself; it is a leap in the darkness of life which believes that man will find what is liberating only when he turns over himself in an active availability to a mystery that he can never fully understand. Such trust is frightening, but necessary if man is ever to realize his basic freedom.

Freedom is a task because it is never given at one moment in full measure. Freedom is a gift, but a gift that is never-ending and never complete in life. Freedom is earned and becomes operative only when the responsibility of life and to all creation is accepted by the individual. Freedom is the constant call to allow the presence of

God's grace as the gift of himself to so permeate the human personality that no area is not affected by the goodness of God.

Freedom is creative since it is never tied down to a system or to categories. The bonds of space and time are broken in the free man as are the confines of a narrow approach to life. The free spirit is the person who glides through life discovering the richness hidden in the ordinary; creativity flourishes as the free person explores the possibilities that are his and the potential of the world of which he is a part. Freedom offers a newness that is hidden only waiting to be revealed.

Conclusion

What can be said of Christian personality and freedom? The believer is a free person beyond the control of law and sin and death when and to the extent that the believer is a spirit-filled person, to the extent that the believer has given himself to the mystery that is God. The task is growing in understanding of self and in this awareness of self a growing in self-disposal as we freely choose the destiny that is given to us. The new law of freedom is exercised concretely, and this implies the particular manifestations that include the concrete love of neighbor. We are most free when we give ourselves actively in love to God through the active gift of love to others and to this world; we are most free when we allow ourselves to be what we are: individual persons who are called to share the mystery that is God, which is the fulfillment of the mystery that is man. In all that he does, the free person gives himself to the good and then he achieves freedom and becomes a person.

SOURCE: John F. O'Grady, *Christian Anthropology: A Meaning for Human Life* (New York: Paulist Press, 1976), pp. 118–123.

25
Self-Discipline
Thomas Merton

Life is a smorgasbord, not a one-course meal. Life presents us with many desirable options from which to choose. If we are so indecisive that we choose nothing, then we starve; if we are so voracious that we attempt to eat everything, we sicken. To partake of life and truly savor it, therefore, demands self-discipline, a training that facilitates self-control, orderly choosing, and development of character.

Human nature has a tendency toward self-indulgence which severs us from our fourfold relationships. Self-discipline is a way to a freedom which consists in being master of oneself and receptive to our relational status. Plainly, we cannot have everything at the same time; we must choose. We must have the courage to surrender one thing in order that the others can come to pass. Self-discipline develops that courage.

For St. Paul, the Christian is like the athlete who must constantly train and practice self-discipline in order to win the race (1 Cor. 9:24–27). In the Gospels, self-discipline and asceticism are presented under the concrete theme of following Jesus:

> If any man wishes to come after me, let him deny himself and take up his cross and follow me. For whoever would save his life will lose it; and whosoever loses his life for my sake and the gospel's will save it (Mark 8:34–35; Matthew 16:24–25; Luke 9:23–24).

Healthy self-discipline is not repression, not contempt for the body and emotions, not world-renouncing asceticism. Rather, self-discipline for the Christian is a conscious self-control, a spirit of non-attachment, a systematic exercise of the Christian life, an overcoming of that which stands in the way of the great commandment: love of God and love of neighbor.

Self-discipline is certainly not a concern peculiar to the monastic life-style; however, our next selection is taken from that context. Thomas Merton was a convert to Catholicism who became a monk in the Trappist order, an order known for its austerity and its members' self-discipline. Merton became an internationally recognized literary figure, having written more than thirty books, including his candid autobiography—a spiritual classic of our time: *The Seven Storey Mountain.* At the age of fifty-four, just before Christmas 1968, Merton died accidentally while attending a dialogue on Western and Oriental monasticism in Bangkok, Thailand. Both his writings and his life speak eloquently of the need and benefits of self-discipline.

The reasons for discipline lie . . . [deep].

St. Paul long ago remarked on the obvious analogy between the training of athletes and the discipline of Christian self-denial. . . . If one "trains" and disciplines his faculties and his whole being, it is in order to deepen and expand their capacity for experience, for awareness, for understanding, for a higher kind of life, a deeper and more authentic life "in Christ" and "in the Spirit." The purpose of discipline is not only moral perfection (development of virtue for its own sake) but self-transcendence, transformation in Christ "from glory to glory, as by the Spirit of the Lord." The death and crucifixion of the old self, the routine man of self-seeking and conventionally social life, leads to the resurrection in Christ of a totally "new man" who is "one Spirit" with Christ. This new man is not just the old man in possession of a legal certificate entitling him to a reward. He is no longer the same, and his reward is precisely this transformation that makes him no longer the isolated subject of a limited reward but "one with Christ," and, in Christ, with all men. The purpose of discipline is then not only to help us "turn on" and understand the inner dimensions of existence, but to transform us in Christ in such a way that we completely transcend our routine existence. (Yet in transcending it, we rediscover its existential value and solidity. Transformation is not a repudiation of ordinary life but its definitive recovery in Christ.)

... "Behold the Bridegroom comes: go out to meet Him!" The need for discipline is the same need for watchfulness, for readiness, as in the parable. The ones who wait for the Lord must have oil in their lamps and lamps must be trimmed. ... It implies the cultivation of certain inner conditions of awareness, of openness, or readiness for the new and the unexpected. Specifically, it implies an openness to, a readiness for what is not normally to be found in an existence where our attention is dissipated and exhausted in other things. ...

... True discipline is interior and personal. It is something more than just learning a certain kind of conduct and possessing coherent religious justifications for that conduct. It is one thing to say that when I make a profound bow I intend to express love and adoration for God, but another to really grow and develop in that love and adoration. ...

... I think we ought to be more conscious of and attentive to the kind of para-monasticism which is very alive in this country. I mean, frankly, movements like the hippies, like the beats before them, like all those who are interested in Yoga and Zen, like (in other respects) the peace movement, the civil rights movement. All these movements have elements that can be called monastic in the sense that they imply a very radical and critical break with ordinary social patterns. They have their asceticism, their "discipline," in the various kinds of sacrifices they make in order to "break" with their own past, with their normal milieu, with the society of their parents, or with a social order with which they violently disagree. ...

... The idea of discipline implies a clear recognition of an elementary human fact: permissiveness is all right if you are content to drift along with a stream that carries you more or less safely by itself. We can to a great extent trust our nature and culture to guide us once we have learned the relatively easy and habitual norms they impose. But this easy permissive drifting existence is bought at a price: it excludes certain other dimensions of life which cannot be found unless to some extent we work hard to discover them. Of course one must always admit of exceptions. There may be people who drift along permissively and who attain an unusual degree of wisdom. But usually you will find that even their apparent permissiveness is the result of a break, a sacrifice of certain easy adjustments and of a conventional role. The man who wants to deepen his existential awareness has to make a break with ordinary existence, and this break is costly. It cannot be made without anguish and suffering. It implies loneliness, and the disorientation of one who has to recognize that the old signposts don't show him his way, and that in fact he has to find the way by himself without a map. . . .

. . . Discipline develops our critical insight and shows us the inadequacy of what we had previously accepted as valid in our religious and spiritual lives. It enables us to abandon and to discard as irrelevant certain kinds of experience which, in the past, meant a great deal to us. It makes us see that what previously served as a real "inspiration" has now become a worn-out routine and that we must go on to something else. It gives us the courage to face the risk and anguish of the break with our previous level of experience. It enables us, in the language of St. John of the Cross, to face the Dark Night in full awareness of our need to be stripped of what formerly gratified and helped us. . . .

SOURCE: Thomas Merton, *Contemplation in a World of Action* (Garden City, New York: Image Books, 1973), pp. 117–119, 123–127, 129.

26
Care of the Body
Carl E. and LaVonne Braaten

Our bodies—short or tall, plump or thin, black or pink—are utterly magnificent creations. Feel the blood course; listen to the heart beat; taste the salt of a tear; observe the hand's complex flexibility. Marvel at the fact that one drop of your blood no bigger than this letter "a" contains 5,000,000 red blood cells which carry oxygen to all tissues of the body; and in that same drop are 5,000 white blood cells which help maintain immunity to infection and resistance against bacteria and foreign particles. It is this body which provides us with an identity; and it is by means of this awe-inspiring body that we are related to each other, to the world around us, and to God.

Fortunately, the radical body-soul dichotomy which has plagued Western civilization is coming to an end. The various heresies that have overemphasized the spiritual to the detriment of the bodily have been laid to rest in the quest to enjoy the bodily and to seek wholeness of personhood. We have been overly concerned with the *spiritual* (ascetical practices and inner states) in our *spirituality.* We have been concerned about the ecstasy of the spirit. Now we are asking about the ecstasy of the body in order to bring about total human development.

We are body-persons, but unfortunately we often forget to express thankfulness for those bodies or to let our bodies worship the Lord along with our "spirit." Our Creator has given us bodies endowed with exquisite beauty and grace. No doubt God expects us to use our bodies not as a hindrance in our progress toward him, not as "weapons of iniquity" in the cause of sin, but rather as "weapons of justice for God" (Romans 6:13).

The story of our creation in Genesis speaks of the goodness of materiality—and of the body. The incarnation absolutely shouts the importance of the body. The resurrection foreshadows the glory destined for the body. The institution of sacraments or sense-signs which affect the body, involve the body, and rely on the body's cooperation is a concrete illustration of the dignity, worth, and necessity of our muscles, bones, and sinews—that which, according to St. Paul, may become the temple of the Holy Spirit.

We never have the right to ruin the health of our bodies—to make sick and diminished persons of ourselves—even in the context of the cross. Although certain levels of asceticism and discipline of the body are at times necessary (witness the champion athlete), generally most of us need to appreciate and enjoy our bodies more, rather than to curb them through debilitating asceticism. We are called not to suppress the energies of the body but to cherish and tend them.

Energy, courage, zest for life, and willingness to undertake arduous endeavors are all bound up with bodily health. Attempting a harmonious balance of exercise, diet, rest, and positive mental attitude is, therefore, a duty of the human body-person, as it certainly is of the Christian who recognizes the material world and the body as precious gifts from the Creator.

Carl and LaVonne Braaten address themselves to Christianity and the role of the body in the following excerpt, taken from their book: *The Living Temple: A Practical Theology of the Body and the Foods of the Earth.* LaVonne is the owner and operator of several health food stores in Illinois; Carl is a Lutheran pastor and professor of theology.

In the body we are individualized and personalized. Yet no one is wholly and only his body. He is always a member of a larger body together with others, as long as he is a living body. The alternative is to become a corpse, no longer capable of encountering others and enjoying bodily relationships. It is by means of the body that we are related to God and to the world around us. It takes on communal-relational meaning. In Paul's use of body language this is especially clear. By his body a person is an individual living in space and time. In his body he can perform the works of sin and evil, this living according to the flesh. But also in his body he can live in a new set of relationships, act on new possibilities. "The body is . . . for the Lord"

(1 Cor. 6:13), Paul said. Believers are united with Christ in a new body alive with the Spirit. This makes all the difference in how they live. Anything that competes with this new orientation of the body in unity with Christ is a sin unto death, like having sex with a prostitute, being circumcised after baptism, or eating meat in heathen temples, etc. For such things make the body a partner of deeds that do not spring from the new life in Christ.

The idea of being united with others in the body of Christ is symbolized for believers in the sacrament of eating bread. Christ took bread, broke it and gave it to his friends, saying, "This is my body" (Matt. 26:26). The body of Christ and sacramental bread become identified. The believer enters into union with Christ by means of the water in baptism and he celebrates that unity by sharing a meal of bread and wine with others. Eating and drinking—bodily events from top to bottom—become the most spiritual transactions in a person's life, and in the common life of a whole people. The people's liturgy is expressed in the ritual body, in eucharistic bread and sacramental wine—mediating the presence of the great Name. The body is the mysterium maximum. Who dare condemn it?

The liturgical claim on the body has direct relevance to its involvements in real life. In Paul's day, as in every period of the church, including our own, there was a group of enthusiastic Christians who, in typical Gnostic fashion, held that they were so caught up in the Spirit, it was quite irrelevant what they did with their bodies. They operated with a kind of realized eschatology, fancying that they had already attained immortality, already in a position of transcendence above the mundane matters of the body. The body clings to the soul like a suit of old clothes ready for the grab bag. But it's so worn and tattered, it doesn't much matter what a person does with it anymore. So forget about the body's sexual purity; forget about holding a job; never mind what you eat. Against these Spirit-enthusiasts Paul said, the body is the real self. It plays a fundamental role in the new age which the Spirit has begun in the body of Christ. The body is redeemed and sanctified as an essential value in the future God has in store for us. Because the body is for the Lord, keep it holy until the parousia. The impending judgment will call each man to account according to the deeds performed in the body.

The enthusiasts at Corinth were scandalized by Paul's inclusion of the body in the sphere of Christ. Since the body for them lacked eschatological validity, there was no reason to care about its ethical meaning. But for Paul the body and spirit are one in the end. He coined the phrase "spiritual body" (*soma pneumaticos*). The body belongs to the eschatological existence. In some way the eternal future of humanity will retain continuity with its bodily basis here and now. The body will be transformed, Paul says, spiritual, resurrected, glorified, but he has no way of telling us what these symbols mean in metaphysical terms. If the body is the necessary condition of communication and relationship here and now, it must also provide the symbolic data for the imagination in speaking of the eternal future of man. We may choose to remain silent, but in any case we have no way of speaking of naked spiritual existence without the body.

The impact of the term "spiritual body" is not metaphysical but ethical. Its payoff is not speculative but practical. As a symbol it affirms our faith in the goodness of the body. God created it good. It is the chosen seat of the Spirit of God and the very medium of our encounter with his Son Jesus Christ. This makes the body an excellent place to enjoy the gift of life. A negative attitude to the body leads to the breakdown of social order. Again Paul carried the argument to the pneumatic enthusiasts at Corinth. They did not discern the body, and so let a class distinction arise between the rich and the poor and between first- and second-class members in the congregation. The notion that God can be approached through mystical experience or esoteric knowledge by gaining distance from our bodies does violence to his real presence in the body to body relationships in the social order. "I was hungry, I was thirsty, I was a stranger, I was naked, I was sick, I was in prison." These are all bodily relationships—food, water, shelter, clothes, medicine. We meet God in the body of such relationships with all our fellowmen. The seed of this concern for justice is respect for the body; the revelation of its diginity is the flesh of Christ; the stage of its enactment is the body of the world; the measure of its health is justice for all its weaker members.

Christians are called to walk the incarnational line in history. They are to be guided by the coming of Christ in the flesh and live according to the Spirit of his body. This does not mean getting all wrapped up in the second coming and guessing about the sequence of events surrounding doomsday. The Jesus-people and the Spirit-people of today are manifesting the same weariness with the world which betrayed the old Christian Gnostics into heresy. Instead of letting the Spirit drive us more deeply into our bodies, where we meet God in his perpetual humanity, spiritual enthusiasts would have us cut our ties with the body and the earth which feeds it. They would have our souls take off into another kind of world, enjoying communion with God at the level of God in heaven, in contrast to the message of the Bible which shows God following the pull of gravity itself, coming down to earth, settling into our human skins, and holding fellowship with us at the level of flesh and blood.

The old Gnosticism is remaking its appearance in Western culture, by imposing exotic varieties of the dualistic traditions of the East. Many Christians are susceptible to the highfalutin' talk about the soul in Eastern mysticism, because the Church has given them to believe that Christianity is essentially a message about the soul, only offering it the best chance of getting saved. A Western scholar once put the question to an old Caledonian islander whether it was not the idea of the soul which Christianity had brought to them. "No," was the unexpected reply, "we already know about that; what you have given to us is the notion of the body."

Why are so many Christians dropping out of the churches and letting themselves get swept up by spiritual winds flowing in from the East? Some may say it is because the churches are not spiritual enough. In fact, the opposite is true; they are not somatic enough. Perhaps they occupy a no-man's-land between body and spirit. We miss the body language of the gospel in the churches; others complain that they miss the excitements of the Spirit. So they are leaving the Church for the Eastern option. We are staying with the Church, demanding in the name of the gospel that it return home to the body.

SOURCE: Carl E. and LaVonne Braaten, *The Living Temple: A Practical Theology of the Body and the Foods of the Earth* (New York: Harper and Row, 1976), pp. 17–20.

27
Leisure
Marie Therese Ruthmann

Technology has mastered the art of saving time but not
the art of spending it. Technology has created vast new
blocks of free time for us all. And we are perplexed. We
move from frantic entertainment to feelings of guilt for
"killing time," to boredom, and to meaninglessness. In a
word, we are being confronted with the challenge of leisure in a way hardly envisioned by past generations.

Leisure is often identified with time—time beyond that
required for existence and subsistence, a time when the
feeling of compulsion should be minimal. Leisure is the
time of opportunity to enlarge human experience as we
reflect on time-past, savor time-present, and dream of
time-future. Leisure is the time to experience myself as a
being with an origin and a destiny—not just an ephemer-
al bubble.

Leisure is also identified as the opposite of work. This
does not imply the denial of work-as-a-blessing, through
which we create ourselves and our world. No, not at all.
But leisure puts work in its proper place. Work is not, as
the workaholic would have us believe, the end of living;
work is only one part of living. Another part is leisure,
that is, slowing down to look at a flower, to chat with a
friend, to pat a dog, to read a few lines from a book, or
simply "to do nothing"—to be removed from the worka-
day world.

Leisure, however, must not be conceived of merely in
relation to time or work. For leisure is most basically an
attitude of mind. This attitude is especially well described
in the last paragraph of the following selection, written
by Sister Marie Therese Ruthmann, V.M.H., who teaches
English and religion at the Academy of the Visitation, St.
Louis.

With these descriptions of leisure in mind, it is well to

recall Jesus' rebuke of Martha—the one who waits so diligently upon him with service, and who became angry at her sister for waiting on the Lord merely by listening to his teaching. Jesus said, "Martha, Martha, you are anxious and troubled about many things." Calm down! Have leisure! "Be still, and know that I am God" (Psalm 46:10). "This is the day which the Lord has made; let us rejoice and be glad in it" (Psalm 118:24). Calm down! Have leisure!

Jesus appreciated leisure. He knew, for example, how to pause in order to admire the splendor of wild flowers. In that splendor he recognized the concern, goodness, and providence of the Creator, which, after all, are the reasons why we can be leisurely.

The Puritan Influence

As devout Puritans, the founding fathers of America were influenced by [an] . . . attitude . . . [of hard] work and activity. Yet when they arrived in the New World, hungry, lonely, and sick, they had need of no other motive than sheer survival in a hostile wilderness to urge them to work. In their case it was not psychological escape or suspicion of leisure but necessity that made them echo St. Paul's dictum: "The man who does not work, does not eat." Yet the word leisure did have unfavorable connotations for them. It was associated with the idleness and luxury pursued at the expense of the lower classes that characterized the aristocratic classes in Europe, a way of life from which the Puritans were very legitimately escaping. Therefore as an extension of European influences, the Puritan frame of reference regarding work and leisure had a marked influence on American culture.

For the Puritan, a useful and responsible life involved devotion to Almighty God centered in the study of Scripture and rooted in work. Through his work the Christian made his response to God. . . . Because the Puritan felt responsible for using the talents God gave him in the work to which he was called, he cultivated such qualities as sobriety, thrift, industry, and punctuality. He frowned upon idleness and debilitating recreational activities which hindered his life as a worker. Though the Puritans approved of "seasonable merriment," they deplored immoderate diversion as a waste of time. If activity required time and energy, it should yield results worth the effort. So instead of divorcing work and pleasure, such occasions as weddings, barn raisings, quilting parties, and cornhuskings became occasions for pleasure as well as cooperative effort for a useful end. Such a view of work could not help but lead to economic success, a fact that led Max Weber and Tawney to their conclusions about the direct relationship between Puritan ethics and the rise of capitalism.

In the eighteenth century, just before the Revolutionary War, a major split occurred in the concern that had united the Puritan founders: the interrelatedness of the individual's spiritual life with its outer forms of work and conduct. Jonathan Edwards, the New England clergyman so prominent in the spiritual revival called the Great Awakening, stressed man's inner spiritual life, his sense of sinfulness, and his total dependence on God. Although man could do nothing to save his soul, he must live a godly and sober life to win possible election. At the same time, Benjamin Franklin, American patriot and patron saint of the industrious, extolled the Puritan virtues of work and thrift in isolation from the faith which contained them. He gave them intrinsic justification as the way to successful life in this world. . . . Since Franklin's time, American politicians and businessmen have continued to praise work and to be suspicious of leisure on the pretext that work is the way to progress and wealth and national greatness. Christian Churches have continued to be equally suspicious of leisure as an immoral use of time. As a result, [some] writers . . . locate present attitudes toward work and leisure more in the utilitarian than in the Puritan philosophy from which it grew. . . .

The Utilitarian Bias

. . . They [utilitarians] live consciously or unconsciously by the principle that only useful activity is valuable, meaningful, and moral. Activity that is not concretely useful to oneself or to others is considered worthless, meaningless, and immoral. . . .

. . . Modern men and women [have] internalized the idea that what is important and worthwhile in life is the profit they may draw from a possession or experience. . . .

The Heresy of Activism

Thus by the time technology might have produced leisure, men's consciences have been so formed against any habits of unprofitable pleasure that even free time has become a guilty burden. People feel morally and psychologically compelled to fill hours now free from work with added tasks in order to justify their idleness. Men work intellectually five days a week at the office and then find some physical pastimes to labor at on week-ends and evenings. Women finish their housework and dash off to get involved in volunteer services or part-time jobs to occupy their time in ways that make them feel useful. When they approach 40 or when all their children are old enough to be in school, most women trade the work of homemaking for that of a career without even considering the available option of leisure. Men and women alike put off some pleasure, such as reading a book, until some work actually requires it; they justify the time spent listening to music because they do so while they are ironing or gardening or working at something else. Children are praised and made to feel good about themselves if they work and attain high grades, if they keep busy cutting the grass or helping with housework, if they earn money at an after-school job. They grow up being made to feel guilty about taking time to think or to dream or simply do nothing. The irony of this situation is that although technology is affording people more and more time free from work, most of them are not truly free to use it because they believe that only work is meaningful. Activism has become a way of life.

Activism as Flight from Self

Psychiatrist Rollo May observes that this activism, the tendency to assume that the more a person is acting, the more he is alive, is really a subtle way of running away from oneself. People keep busy all the time to cover up anxiety, to substitute for self-awareness. . . .

. . . Unexpected or forced inactivity, whether it is recuperating from illness or waiting at an airport or in a doctor's office or "enjoying" a vacation, produces varying degrees of uneasiness, restlessness, and frustration.

This comparatively new attitude toward effort and work as an end in themselves may be the most important psychological change which has happened to man since the Middle Ages. In every society man has had to work in order to live. Some societies solved this problem by means of slaves who did the work while free men occupied themselves with nobler activity than work. In medieval society, too, work was unequally distributed, but then the attitude toward work was not that of producing a commodity to be sold. Only modern society seems to live to work. . . .

The Leisure Attitude

. . . Modern man acts as if his sole purpose in life is to do: he forgets or does not know how simply to be. Yet an integrated life is both receptive and active. What will enable him to be free to make a more contemplative response to life? If modern man truly desires a more balanced and meaningful life, then he must understand and cultivate leisure.

But what is leisure? One of the first helpful distinctions concerning true leisure is that it is not primarily concerned with time at all. Free time, time left over from work, is in itself vacant and faceless. It has no innate capacity or magic power to give joy or pleasure or meaning. Free time is only potentially leisure. More than any quantity, leisure is a quality of life as a whole. It is a state of being, an attitude that sees time not so much as a commodity to be exploited as an opportunity to be. . . .

Inner Conflict: The Necessity To Trust

. . . It is time to rediscover the meaning of one's being as man playing as well as man working and thus a more balanced life.

This will entail a real process of conversion in a person who has previously valued himself and sought the esteem and love of others mainly in terms of his work. What is necessary first of all is an attitude of basic trust that he is of value, good, and lovable simply because he is. Basically this is what faith in God is: The trust that God loves man just as he is, that he does not have to merit God's love or live up to expectations. To have this faith in God and to be able to have this basic self-esteem, a person has to have experienced another human being's acceptance of him as a good person in himself and not for what he can achieve or produce. . . .

The Necessity To Pray

. . . The inner conflicts and anxiety that urge men to more and more work and activity, manual and intellectual, can be an invitation from God to "be still" and reflect on ourselves and our lives in His presence. Swiss psychiatrist Paul Tournier observes that to rediscover the creative imagination, to see the problems that are raised in life and that men skirt without confronting, to understand them, to reflect on them and to resolve them, men must know how to stop and observe moments of contemplation. . . .

... It must be noted, however, that prayer is not utilitarian. It is a time when one can simply be oneself, not trying to be someone else, and not striving to measure up to some goal. It is not a duty but a relationship. It is not a means to inner harmony, but, paradoxically, that is exactly the effect it has. The East seems to have understood this far better than the West. Today many people are borrowing insights from ancient religions such as Taoism and Buddhism that stress contemplation, creative inaction, the attempt to experience God and the world in a pre-cognitive, intuitive way, and they are finding that their lives have more meaning and fewer conflicts.

The Necessity To Take Time

This lived experience of East and West seems to indicate that in addition to a basic attitude of trust and self-esteem, the next step away from a work-orientation is simply the decision to take time. If a compulsive worker thinks of time he would like to have for leisure as something he will get after work, he will never get it. If, on the other hand, he thinks of the time he needs for inner growth as something he can get in his busiest moments if only he takes it, then he will take the time, no matter how busy he is. For such a person, life has frequently become a relentless schedule. To know himself, to find some sort of orientation in the world, it may be necessary to ignore the schedule, to do as he likes for a while, to do nothing but look and listen. The only way to develop a sense of leisure is to be leisurely. This will be difficult for a generous person who feels morally constrained to be involved and useful even to the point of being overworked and fatigued. If he is ever to take time, however, he will have to cultivate the ability to say no to many useful services without feeling guilty about it. The recognition that in order to build up the kingdom of God a Christian is called not merely to create something outside himself but to create himself is powerful motivation. What people need for this is not necessarily more time but an inner attitude of contemplative celebration of the time they have. ...

Conclusion

In Psalm 46 the Psalmist has God say: "Be still and know that I am God." Be still—have leisure—and know that life has not only purpose but meaning. What, then, is leisure? It is freedom for a playful response of the whole person to God, other persons, and the world. Paradoxically, it is the origin and ground of all creative work. It is the ability to be still, to transcend anxieties and cares, to accept oneself and be at peace with oneself and all creation. It is the serenity to rest in intrinsically meaningful activity: in contemplative listening and intuitive rejoicing. It is re-creation of the spirit and body, re-creation of the mind and heart. It is wisdom to live wholly and holily in each present moment, accepting it from the hands of a loving Father and celebrating it with thanksgiving as a gift. Leisure is an attitude of "waiting upon" meaning without knowing what it will be, an openness for the ever-unfolding adventure and surprise of life. Since leisure consists in experience rather than information, all the time that is necessary for it is the present moment.

SOURCE: Marie Therese Ruthmann, "Celebrating Leisure Today," *Review for Religious* 32 (May 1973), pp. 544–548, 550–552, 556.

28
Death
Elisabeth Kübler Ross et al., eds.

Did you know that each year about 325,000 Americans die from cancer? Heart attack alone kills about 2,000 people daily in our country. And with each death, many others grieve. Yet in the midst of these realities, ours is a death-denying society. Thoughts of mortality are shunned; the bereaved are isolated; the spectre of death in our sick and elderly is ignored within the sterile walls of hospitals and with the cosmetic masks of funerals.

The following selection, however, insists that through an acceptance of our finiteness, "death [becomes] the key to the door of life":

> When we know and understand completely that our time on this earth is limited, and that we have no way of knowing when it will be over, then we must live each day as if it were the only one we had.

From the Judaeo-Christian perspective death itself is somewhat of a mystery and a paradox. The Old Testament writers speak of death almost as a reward for a faithful life (Job 42:17); and yet death is also feared and rejected, as if the dead were beyond God's remembrance and care (Psalm 88:6). Paul sums up the paradox for Christians in the fifteenth chapter of his First Letter to the Corinthians. He argues that although death is the sting of sin, we overcome sin and death by our identification with the risen Christ. This, of course, is a dominant Christian theme.

Physical death, however, is just one aspect of dying. Paul himself recognizes that in a very real sense we are constantly dying: to the moment, to our old selves, to the roles that others choose for us. We are constantly experiencing various and often subtle losses, and then grief, and then, ideally, hope.

Christianity helps us to recognize this loss-grief-hope continuum in our lives. It tells us that we are never alone; that even in our losses and grief, God is present; that life as we presently experience it is not an absolute. Christianity facilitates reflection on our own death and teaches us that we will be better able to live life because of that reflection. The denial of death—and living as if "I will live forever here on earth"—often results in people living purposeless lives. Coming to terms with death enables us to prioritize those lives. Sometimes nothing but the death of a loved one and/or reflection on our own death will remind us we are alive and full of love.

The following excerpts are taken from the book, *Death: The Final Stage of Growth,* edited by Joseph and Laurie Braga, and Elisabeth Kübler-Ross who is a psychiatrist and world-renowned authority on death. We wish to point out that the Bragas and Ross are not writing as theologians nor even as Christians. We, your editors, strongly believe that in the art of Christian personning, Christians must recognize and incorporate the valuable insights about life which come from all quarters.

Death is a subject that is evaded, ignored, and denied by our youth-worshipping, progress-oriented society. It is almost as if we have taken on death as just another disease to be conquered. But the fact is that death is inevitable. We will all die; it is only a matter of time. Death is as much a part of human existence, of human growth and development, as being born. It is one of the few things in life we can count on, that we can be assured will occur. Death is not an enemy to be conquered or a prison to be escaped. It is an integral part of our lives that gives meaning to human existence. It sets a limit on our time in this life, urging us on to do something productive with that time as long as it is ours to use.

. . . [Even] when you're dying, if you're fortunate enough to have some prior warning (other than that we all have all the time if we come to terms with our finiteness), you get your final chance to grow, to become more truly who you really are, to become more fully human. But you don't need to nor should you wait until death is at your doorstep before you start to really live. If you can begin to see death as an invisible, but friendly, companion on your life's journey—gently reminding you not to wait till tomorrow to do what you mean to do—then you can learn to *live* your life rather than simply passing through it.

Whether you die at a young age or when you are older is less important than whether you have lived the years you have had. One person may live more in eighteen years than another does in eighty. By living, we do not mean frantically accumulating a range and quantity of experience valued in fantasy by others. Rather, we mean living each day as if it is the only one you have. We mean finding a sense of peace and strength to deal with life's disappointments and pain while always striving to discover vehicles to make more accessible, to increase and sustain the joys and delights of life. One such vehicle is learning to focus on some of the things you have learned to tune out—to notice and take joy in the budding of new leaves in the spring, to wonder at the beauty of the sun rising each morning and setting each night, to take comfort in the smile or touch of another person, to watch with amazement the growth of a child, and to share in children's wonderfully "uncomplexed," enthusiastic, and trusting approach to living. To live.

To rejoice at the opportunity of experiencing each new day is to prepare for one's ultimate acceptance of death. For it is those who have not really lived—who have left issues unsettled, dreams unfulfilled, hopes shattered, and who have let the real things in life (loving and being loved by others, contributing in a positive way to other people's happiness and welfare, finding out what things are really you) pass them by—who are most reluctant to die. It is never too late to start living and growing. This is the message delivered each year in Dickens' "Christmas Carol"—even old Scrooge, who has spent years pursuing a life without love or meaning, is able, through his willing it, to change the road he's on. Growing is the human way of living, and death is the final stage in the development of human beings. For life to be valued every day, not simply near to the time of anticipated death, one's own inevitable death must be faced and accepted. We must allow death to provide a context for our lives, for in it lies the meaning of life and the key to our growth.

Think about your own death. How much time and energy have you put into examining your feelings, beliefs, hopes, and fears about the end of your life? What if you were told you had a limited time to live? Would it change the way you're presently conducting your life? Are you afraid of dying? Of death? Can you identify the sources of your fears? Consider the death of someone you love. What would you talk about to a loved one who was dying? How would you spend

your time together? Are you prepared to cope with all the legal details of the death of a relative? Have you talked with your family
about death and dying? Are there things, emotional and practical,
that you would feel a need to work out with your parents, children,
siblings before your own death or theirs? Whatever the things are
that would make your life more personally meaningful before you
die—do them now, because you are going to die; and you may not
have the time or energy when you get your final notice. . . .

There is no need to be afraid of death. It is not the end of the
physical body that should worry us. Rather, our concern must be to
live while we're alive—to release our inner selves from the spiritual
death that comes with living behind a facade designed to conform to
external definitions of who and what we are. Every individual human
being born on this earth has the capacity to become a unique and
special person unlike any who has ever existed before or will ever exist again. But to the extent that we become captives of culturally defined role expectations and behaviors—stereotypes, not ourselves—
we block our capacity for self-actualization. We interfere with our
becoming all that we can be.

Death is the key to the door of life. It is through accepting the
finiteness of our individual existences that we are enabled to find the
strength and courage to reject those extrinsic roles and expectations
and to devote each day of our lives—however long they may be—to
growing as fully as we are able. We must learn to draw on our inner
resources, to define ourselves in terms of the feedback we receive
from our own internal valuing system rather than trying to fit ourselves into some ill-fitting stereotyped role.

It is the denial of death that is partially responsible for people
living empty, purposeless lives; for when you live as if you'll live forever, it becomes too easy to postpone the things you know that you
must do. You live your life in preparation for tomorrow or in remembrance of yesterday, and meanwhile, each today is lost. In contrast, when you fully understand that each day you awaken could be
the last you have, you take the time that day to grow, to become
more of who you really are, to reach out to other human beings.

There is an urgency that each of you, no matter how many days
or weeks or months or years you have to live, commit yourself to
growth. We are living in a time of uncertainty, anxiety, fear, and de-
spair. It is essential that you become aware of the light, power, and
strength within each of you, and that you learn to use those inner
resources in service of your own and others' growth. The world is in
desperate need of human beings whose own level of growth is suffi-

cient to enable them to learn to live and work with others cooperatively and lovingly, to care for others—not for what those others can do for you or for what they think of you, but rather in terms of what you can do for them. If you send forth love to others, you will receive in return the reflection of that love; because of your loving behavior, you will grow, and you will shine a light that will brighten the darkness of the time we live in—whether it is in a sickroom of a dying patient, on the corner of a ghetto street in Harlem, or in your own home.

Humankind will survive only through the commitment and involvement of individuals in their own and others' growth and development as human beings. This means development of loving and caring relationships in which all members are as committed to the growth and happiness of the others as they are to their own. Through commitment to personal growth individual human beings will also make their contribution to the growth and development— the evolution—of the whole species to become all that humankind can and is meant to be. Death is the key to that evolution. For only when we understand the real meaning of death to human existence will we have the courage to become what we are destined to be.

When human beings understand their place in the universe, they will become able to grow to assume that place. But the answer is not in words on this page. The answer is within you. You can become a channel and a source of great inner strength. But you must give up everything in order to gain everything. What must you give up? All that is not truly you; all that you have chosen without choosing and value without evaluating, accepting because of someone else's extrinsic judgment, rather than your own; all your self-doubt that keeps you from trusting and loving yourself or other human beings. What will you gain? Only your own true self; a self who is at peace, who is able to truly love and be loved, and who understands who and what he is meant for. But you can be yourself only if you are no one else. You must give up "their" approval, whoever they are, and look to yourself for evaluation of success and failure, in terms of your own level of aspiration that is consistent with your values. Nothing is simpler and nothing is more difficult.

Where can you find the strength and courage to reject those outer definitions of yourself and choose, instead, your own?

It is all within you if you look and are not afraid. Death can show us the way, for when we know and understand completely that our time on this earth is limited, and that we have no way of knowing when it will be over, then we must live each day as if it were the only one we had. We must take the time, now, to begin—one step at a time, at a pace that makes us not afraid, but rather eager, to take the next step, to grow into ourselves. If you practice life with compassion, love, courage, patience, hope, and faith, you will be rewarded by an ever increasing consciousness of the help that can come forth if only you look within yourself for strength and guidance. When human beings "find a place of stillness and quiet at the highest level of which they are capable, then the heavenly influences can pour into them, recreate them, and use them for the salvation of humankind."

Death is the final stage of growth in this life. There is no total death. Only the body dies. The self or spirit, or whatever you may wish to label it, is eternal. You may interpret this in any way that makes you comfortable.

If you wish, you may view the eternal essence of your existence in terms of the impact your every mood and action has on those you touch, and then, in turn, on those they touch, and on and on—even long after your life span is completed. You will never know, for example, the rippling effects of the smile and words of encouragement you give to other human beings with whom you come in contact.

You may be more comfortable and comforted by a faith that there is a source of goodness, light, and strength greater than any of us individually, yet still within us all, and that each essential self has an existence that transcends the finiteness of the physical and contributes to that greater power.

Death, in this context, may be viewed as the curtain between the existence that we are conscious of and one that is hidden from us until we raise that curtain. Whether we open it symbolically in order to understand the finiteness of the existence we know, thus learning to live each day the best we can, or whether we open it in actuality when we end that physical existence is not the issue. What is important is to realize that whether we understand fully why we are here or what will happen when we die, it is our purpose as human beings to grow—to look within ourselves to find and build upon that source of peace and understanding and strength which is our inner selves, and to reach out to others with love, acceptance, patient guidance, and hope for what we all may become together.

In order to be at peace, it is necessary to feel a sense of history— that you are both part of what has come before and part of what is yet to come. Being thus surrounded, you are not alone; and the sense of urgency that pervades the present is put in perspective: Do not frivolously use the time that is yours to spend. Cherish it, that each day may bring new growth, insight, and awareness. Use this growth not selfishly, but rather in service of what may be, in the future tide of time. Never allow a day to pass that did not add to what was understood before. Let each day be a stone in the path of growth. Do not rest until what was intended has been done. But remember—go as slowly as is necessary in order to sustain a steady pace; do not expend energy in waste. Finally, do not allow the illusory urgencies of the immediate to distract you from your vision of the eternal. . . .

SOURCE: Elisabeth Kübler-Ross *et al.,* eds., "Foreword" and "Omega" in *Death: The Final Stage of Growth* (Englewood Cliffs: Prentice-Hall, 1975) pp. x–xii and 164–167.